HOW TO STUDY LAW

HOW TO STUDY LAW
8th edition

ANTHONY BRADNEY, LL.B., B.A., FAcSS, FRSA
Professor of Law,
Keele University

FIONA COWNIE, B.A., LL.B., LL.M., FAcSS, FRSA
Barrister, Professor of Law,
Keele University

JUDITH MASSON, M.A., Ph.D., FAcSS
Professor of Socio-Legal Studies,
University of Bristol

ALAN C. NEAL, LL.B., LL.M., D.G.L.S.
Barrister, Professor of Law,
University of Warwick

DAVID NEWELL, LL.B., M.Phil.
Solicitor,
Director, The Newspaper Society

SWEET & MAXWELL

 THOMSON REUTERS

Published in 2017 by Thomson Reuters (Professional) UK Limited, trading as Sweet & Maxwell.
Registered in England & Wales. Company number 1679046.
Registered office 5 Canada Square, Canary Wharf, London E14 5AQ.

For further information on our products and services, visit
www.sweetandmaxwell.co.uk

Typeset by Servis Filmsetting Ltd, Stockport, Cheshire
Printed in Great Britain by CPI Group (UK) Ltd, Croydon, CR0 4YY

No natural forests were destroyed to make this product; only farmed
timber was used and re-planted.

A CIP catalogue record for this book is available from the British Library.

ISBN 978-0-414-06153-8

Thomson Reuters and the Thomson Reuters logo are trademarks of Thomson Reuters.
Sweet & Maxwell® is a registered trademark of Thomson Reuters (Professional) UK Limited.

Contents

Acknowledgments

The authors and publishers would like to thank those organisations who have allowed their copyrighted materials to be reproduced as examples throughout this book. Grateful acknowledgment is made to the following authors and publishers for permission to quote from their works: F. Cownie et al., "English Legal System in Context", 4th edn (2007), by permission of Oxford University Press. R. Moorhead and V. Henley, "Professional Minimalism? The Ethical Consciousness of Commercial Lawyers" (2015) 42 Journal of Law and Society 389, © Journal of Law and Society, © Cardiff University Law School, by permission of John Wiley & Sons. "R v Jackson [1999] 1 All E.R.", reproduced by permission of RELX (UK) Limited, trading as LexisNexis. "Re B (A Child) In re B (A Child) (Wrongful Removal: Orders against Non-Parties)" [2014] EWCA Civ 843, by permission of ICLR (The Incorporated Council of Law Reporting for England and Wales)'.

All efforts were made to contact the copyright holders and grateful acknowledgment is made to I.C.L.R., TSO, BAILII and Westlaw UK, amongst others for their permissions.

All extracted materials are represented in the format and with the correct content at the time of writing the book and are subject to change.

The authors would like to acknowledge the assistance provided by Patrick Greenhalgh, of the Careers and Employability unit at Keele University, in relation to the contents of Appendix I.

Preface

A new law student is faced with a potentially bewildering variety of sources of law. A recent case mentioned in a lecture might be found in a database of law reports, a printed report, or a website providing access to recent court judgments. There might be journal articles or newspaper reports that discuss the case. The text of an Act can be found in a number of different ways, using both online sources and editions of statutes found in a law library. It can be difficult to know where to start. This book aims to help you make effective use of the law resources to which you have access. Online sources are placed alongside traditional print sources in each of the chapters of the book and their use explained, in order that you can make the best possible use of both.

In a sense, this book is a labour-saving device. Use it as a reference throughout your time as a student, or indeed thereafter, should you decide to go into legal practice. Although this new edition can be used as a textbook associated with a particular course it can also be used as a reference aid to be consulted whenever you have a problem. Consequently, you might use the book selectively, referring to those sections which are useful at a particular point in your studies, or when recommended to look up a case, statute or issue by a member of the teaching staff. Equally you may find the book to be of particular use when you are preparing for assessments for one of the modules that you are studying.

Victoria Fisher, one of the original authors of this book, died at a very young age. An annual prize essay in her name, on the subject of women and law, was established after her death. For details of the prize contact the School of Law at the University of Leicester (*http://www2.le.ac.uk/ departments/law*).

Part 1

▶ 1
Sources of the law

LAW AND LEGAL INSTITUTIONS

The first question to answer is "what is law?" Most laws are not about something dramatic like murder but are, rather, about the everyday details of ordinary life. Every time a purchase is made, a contract under state law is created. Both parties make promises about what they will do; one to hand over the goods, one to pay the price. In this and other ways, everybody is involved in law every day of their lives. In many instances people are free to make their own choices about the rules that govern their lives. If they want to join a club, a religion or a company and be bound by its rules that is a matter for them. Some people regard these rules as being law just like the law that the state creates. This idea is known as *legal pluralism*. However the kind of law that comes from the state is what we most frequently think about when we think about law. University courses involving law focus on this type of law and that is what this book is about. ▶ 1.1

    There are a number of generally acknowledged sources of English law. Some are more obvious than others. Thus, "the Queen in Parliament" (the House of Commons, the House of Lords and the monarch) is a vital source of modern English law. Here proposals for legislation (*Bills*) are presented to, debated by, and voted upon by the House of Commons and the House of Lords, finally receiving the assent of the monarch and thus becoming legislation (*Statutes* or *Acts*). However judges are also significant sources of law, partly because the English legal system places great emphasis upon judgments in previous legal cases as guidance for future judicial decision-making and partly because, in some instances, judges can themselves make law. There are, however, less obvious sources of English law. Some are direct: for example, in some circumstances, at the time of writing, the European Union may make law for England and Wales. Others are more indirect: thus the customs of a particular trade may be incorporated into the law by the judges or Parliament or international law (the law between states) may be a basis for national law.

    All of the above are sources of *legal rules*. What precisely it is that is meant by the term legal rules is a subject much debated by philosophers of law. Generally speaking, when the term is used it indicates that a particular course of action should, or should not, be followed. Legal rules are said to be *binding*. This means if they are not followed some action in the courts may result.

    It will suffice for present purposes if we consider just two of these sources of law: Parliament and the judiciary. In so doing, we will discover the central positions occupied within the English legal system by *statute law* and *judge-made law*. There is a further explanation of international law and the law of the European Union in Chapter 2.

PARLIAMENT

1.2 ▶ Parliament creates law but not all the law that is created through Parliament is of the same kind. We need, in particular, to distinguish between various levels of legislation.

The legislation with which most people are familiar are statutes. Bills proposed in Parliament become Acts. These Acts may either be *General* or *Personal and Local*. Both of these are sometimes known as *primary legislation*. General Acts apply to everybody, everywhere within the legal system. In this context it is important to remember that there are several different legal systems within the UK; one for England and Wales, one for Scotland and one for Northern Ireland. Sometimes the law in Wales is different to that in England and some people argue that a Welsh legal system is either in the process of being created or already exists. Some Acts apply to all the legal systems; many apply only to one or two of them.

Personal and local Acts apply either to particular individuals, institutions or, more usually, to particular areas. Thus, before divorce was part of the general law, it was only possible to get a divorce by Act of Parliament. The most common example of local legislation is that which applies to individual cities. The law in Leicester is sometimes not the same as the law in London. General legislation is much more common than personal and local legislation.

A legal rule in a statute can only be changed by new legislation. Judges interpret statutes but they do not have the power to change them. Any statute, no matter how important it seems, can be changed in the same way as any other.

Most legislation consists of a direct statement about how people should behave or indicates the consequences of certain behaviour. For example, a statute may define a crime and say what the punishment will be for that crime. Sometimes Parliament cannot decide exactly what the law should be on a particular point. It may not have the necessary expertise or it may be that the area is one where frequent changes are needed. In such cases Parliament may pass an Act giving somebody else the power to make law in the appropriate area. Such power is often given to government ministers or to local authorities. This is the most common example of what is known as *delegated* or *secondary legislation*. A person or body to whom legislative power is delegated cannot, as can Parliament, make law about anything. The Act (sometimes called *the parent Act*) will determine the area in which law can be made. It may say something about the content of the law but the details of that law will be left to the person or body to whom legislative power is delegated. They may also have the power to change that law from time to time. Most delegated legislation is published as a statutory instrument. Although people are frequently unaware of this type of legislation it is very important, affecting most people's lives. For example, much of the social security system is based on delegated legislation.

The final thing that we have to consider is the range of directives, circulars, and guidance notes produced by various State agencies and bodies such as HMRC. Some of these documents bind the people to whom they are addressed to behave in particular ways. Many, however, are not legally binding. They do not compel people to do things in the way that statutes or statutory instruments do. Even so, such documents are often very influential. In practice officials receiving them may always act in the way they indicate. Thus we might consider them all as almost equivalent to legislation.

In Chapter 4 you will find an explanation of how to find statutes and statutory instruments. In Chapter 5 there is an explanation of how you read them to find out where the law stands about something. The methods that the judiciary use to decide how a particular legislative provision is to be interpreted are explained in Chapter 7.

JUDGES, COURTS AND TRIBUNALS

Precedents

Not all legal rules are laid down in an Act of Parliament or some other piece of legislation. A ▶ 1.3 number of legal rules are found in the statements of judges made in the course of deciding cases brought before them. Rules that ultimately come from judicial decisions, rather than from legislation, make what is called the *common law*. A common law rule has as much force as a rule derived from statute. Many important areas of English law, such as contract, tort, criminal law, land law and constitutional law have their origins in common law. An explanation of the different divisions of law is to be found in Chapter 2. Some of the earliest common law rules still survive, though many have been supplemented or supplanted by statute. Common law rules are still being made today, though, as a source of new legal rules, common law is much less important than statute.

Strictly speaking, the term common law is confined to rules that have been developed entirely by judicial decisions. It excludes new rules made by judges when they interpret statutes. Most decisions made by judges now involve, at least in part, interpreting statutes. The term *case law* covers both kinds of decisions.

The application of case law is easiest to understand when the issue presently before the court has been raised in some previous analogous case. In such a situation the court will look to see if there is a potential applicable rule in the reports of previously decided cases. Then they will decide whether they have to, or should, apply that rule. It is therefore vital that accurate and comprehensive records be kept of past court decisions and judicial pronouncements. Thus the importance of the numerous and varied series of law reports can be appreciated. Anybody entering a law library in England can hardly help being impressed at the volume of materials falling within this category of Law Reports. Row upon row of bound volumes, containing the judgments in thousands of past cases, dominate the holdings of any major English law library. In the modern era cases are not only published in printed form. They are also published electronically, either by the courts themselves or by various commercial publishers.

More information about the various kinds of Law Reports and how to use them can be found in Chapter 4.

Not every judgment in every case or every part of a judgment is of equal importance in terms of the creation of law. The weight that is to be given to a judgment as an indication of what future judicial decisions will be depends upon two things. One is the level of the court in which that case was decided. In English law there is a principle of a *hierarchy of precedents*. Judgments given by superior courts in the hierarchy are binding on inferior courts; these judgments create a precedent. The second is whether the part of the judgment that is under consideration is the ratio of the judgment or whether it is obiter dicta. An explanation of the hierarchy of precedents and the rules for determining whether something is ratio or obiter in a judgment is to be found in Chapter 6.

Courts

Cases are decided in courts or tribunals. We look at what tribunals are in the section below. ▶ 1.4 Different kinds of legal disputes are decided in different kinds of courts. Sometimes it is possible to bring a legal dispute before two or more different kinds of court. In some situations, once a court has given judgment, it is possible to appeal against that judgment to another court. Some courts only hear appeals.

The highest court in the English legal system is the Supreme Court, formerly known as the House of Lords. Cases in the Supreme Court are normally heard by five judges (called Justices) but

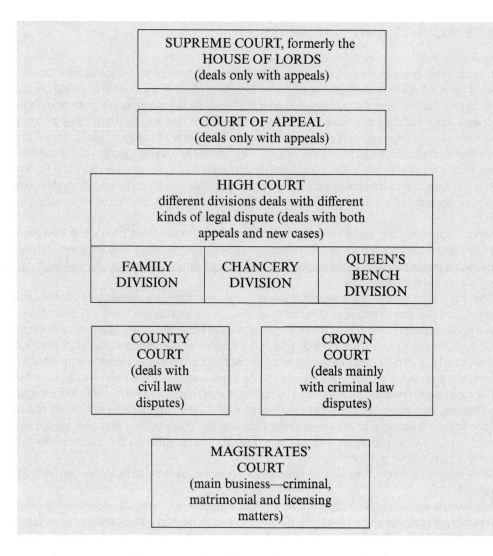

cases involving more than five Justices are becoming increasingly common. Because there is more than one Justice in a case before the Supreme Court the decision may be a majority one.

The Privy Council has a varied jurisdiction. It includes hearing appeals from courts in some Commonwealth countries. Its decisions are not technically binding on courts within the English legal system but, because the judges in the Privy Council are mainly the same as the Justices in the Supreme Court, its decisions are highly influential within the courts in the English legal system.

The court below the Supreme Court is the Court of Appeal. Like the Supreme Court the Court of Appeal has jurisdiction over virtually every area of law. Cases in the Court of Appeal are usually heard by three judges.

The court below the Court of Appeal is the High Court. Both the Supreme Court and the Court of Appeal are basically appellate courts. They hear appeals about the decisions of other lower courts. However the High Court has both an original jurisdiction, that is to say it is a place where a case is first heard there, and an appellate jurisdiction. The High Court is divided into three different Divisions. In practice these Divisions function as though they were separate courts. The Chancery Division mainly hears cases that are concerned with mortgages, the sale of land, the administration of estates of deceased persons or other probate business. The Family Division hears cases about matrimonial matters, including civil partnerships, and matters relating to children. The Queen's Bench Division is the largest of the three Divisions and has a much wider jurisdiction than the other two Divisions. Its jurisdiction includes, amongst other things, judicial review (broadly cases challenging the decisions of bodies with statutory powers such as government departments), criminal law, the law of tort and the law of contract.

None of the courts below the High Court create precedents; that is to say that none of their decisions create legal rules that are binding on other courts. This is not to say that these courts are unimportant. They hear more cases when they first come to court than the High Court does. For most people if they have a case come to court it will be to a court below the High Court. In terms of the operation of the legal system it is the courts below the High Court that matter most. However, most law courses at university are concerned, at least in part, with the analysis of legal rules. This means that courts below the High Court are rarely mentioned in these courses.

The courts immediately below the High Court are the County Court and the Crown Court. The County Court has a civil jurisdiction whilst the Crown Court has a mainly criminal jurisdiction, dealing with the more serious criminal offences. In the Crown Court cases are decided by a judge and a lay jury comprised of 12 people randomly selected from the population at large.

The lowest court in the English legal system is the magistrates' court. Judges who are legally qualified preside in the other courts within the English legal system. However, in the magistrates' court decisions are mostly made by magistrates who are lay people. They receive only a very minimal training in law. Legally qualified clerks advise them. Magistrates' courts are often thought of as courts with a criminal jurisdiction. However, whilst it is true that magistrates' courts do deal with a very large number of minor criminal cases, dealing with approximately 98 per cent of all criminal cases heard each year, they also have a significant civil jurisdiction, dealing with, amongst other things, some family law matters and licensing decisions.

Tribunals

Courts are not the only state institutions that hear cases and make legal decisions. Tribunals have a very similar role to that of the courts. Their hearings tend to be more informal and their decisions tend to be about less serious matters than cases that are heard in court. Tribunal cases are usually decided by a panel comprising of a legally qualified chairperson, who is now oftencalled a judge, and two other people who have knowledge of the area that the tribunal is concerned with. Thus, for example, in an Employment Tribunal the panel might consist of an Employment Judge, a trade union official and someone who is an employer. Tribunals have their own appellate system. Most decisions of tribunals will not constitute a precedent and they will not be reported in the way that decisions of the higher courts are. There are, however, exceptions to this such as the Employment Appeal Tribunal.

▶ 1.5

COMMON LAW AND EQUITY

In the section above the term *common law* is used as a synonym for rules of law derived from judicial decisions rather than statute. This is the most common way in which the phrase is used. However, another sense of the word is as an antonym to *equity*. English law has deep historical

▶ 1.6

roots. The opposition of common law and equity refers to the system of rules that originally developed in different courts within the legal system. Common law rules arose first. Later, these rules were seen as being over-formal and concerned too much with the way a case was presented rather than with the justice in the issues at stake. Thus a less strict system of equitable rules was developed. In time, the rules of equity also became formalised. Eventually, the different courts were merged and now all courts can apply both the rules of common law and equity.

▶ 2
Divisions of law

INTRODUCTION

Not all legal rules are of the same type. Legal rules can be divided up in many different ways. This ▶ 2.1 chapter introduces some common ways of classifying law. They show differences in purpose, in origin and form, in the consequences when the rules are breached, and in matters of procedure, remedies and enforcement. The divisions described below are of the broadest kind. One kind of division of legal rules has already been introduced, that between statute and case or common law. This division and the others now described overlap. For example, the legal rule defining murder originates in common law, not statute. It is a rule of criminal law rather than civil law; and of national law rather than international law.

CRIMINAL AND CIVIL LAW

One of the most fundamental divisions in law is the division between criminal and civil law. ▶ 2.2 Newcomers to the study of law tend to assume that criminal law occupies the bulk of a lawyer's caseload and of a law student's studies. This is an interesting by-product of the portrayal of the legal system by the media. Criminal law weighs very lightly in terms of volume when measured against civil law. There are many more rules of civil law than there are of criminal law; more court cases involve breach of the civil law than involve breach of the criminal law. Law degree students will find that criminal law is generally only one subject out of twelve or more subjects in a three-year law degree, although some criminal offences may be referred to in other courses.

Criminal law means the law relating to crime. Civil law can be taken to mean all the other legal rules within the legal system. The distinction relies not so much on the nature of the conduct that is the object of a legal rule but in the nature of the proceedings and the sanctions that may follow. Some kinds of conduct give rise to criminal liability, some to civil liability and some to both civil and criminal liability.

The seriousness of the conduct does not necessarily determine the type of liability to which it gives rise; conduct that is contrary to the criminal law is not always "worse" than conduct that is against the civil law. Few people would consider every criminal offence a moral wrong (except, perhaps, in the sense that every breach of the law will be thought by some to be a moral wrong). Equally, some actions that are purely breaches of the civil law might be considered breaches of morality. If you breach your contract you break a promise. Nor is harm, in the sense of damage done to individuals, something that is always found to a greater degree in the criminal law as compared with the civil law. The person who "speeds" at 31 miles per hour on an empty road in broad daylight breaches the criminal law. The company that fails to pay for the goods that it has bought, thereby bankrupting another company, commits only a breach of the civil law. Who has done the greater harm? Concepts of morality have had some influence on the development of English law but historical accident, political policy and pragmatic considerations have played just as important a part in developing our law.

Some conduct which might be considered "criminal" by many people gives rise in law only to civil liability or to no liability at all and some conduct which you may consider "harmless" may rise to either criminal or civil liability. It will be easier to see that "harm", "morality" and the division between criminal and civil law do not follow any clear pattern if you consider some fictitious examples. In considering them, ask yourself whether or not the conduct described should give rise to any legal liability; if it should, what form should that liability take and what should the legal consequences be which flow from the conduct described? Should any of the people be compensated for the harm done to them and, if so, by whom and for what? Should any of the characters be punished and, if so, for what reason and how? Who should decide whether or not legal proceedings of any variety should be instigated against any of the individuals? The probable legal consequences that follow from each example are found at the end of the chapter. Do not look at these until you have thought about the examples yourself.

Examples

1. *Norman drinks 5 pints of beer as he does each day. His car suffers a puncture and, as a consequence, he drives into a queue at the bus station injuring a young woman and her child.*
2. *Meena, who is an accountant, regularly takes recreational drugs.*
3. *Sue, who is pregnant, lives with Chris. She smokes 50 cigarettes a day. Sue is also carrying on an occasional affair with Richard.*
4. *Robert agrees to pay Usha, a professional decorator, £5000 if she paints his house. She completes the work to a very high standard. Robert, who is a millionaire, refuses to pay her.*

Even when a person's actions clearly infringe either the criminal law or civil law, it does not necessarily mean that any actual legal consequences will follow. In criminal and civil cases persons with the legal right to take any legal action have a discretion as to whether or not they initiate legal proceedings. There is a difference between *liability* and *proceedings*. Conduct gives rise to liability. It is for someone else to decide whether or not to take the matter to court by starting proceedings.

In criminal proceedings a *prosecutor* prosecutes the *defendant*. The case is heard in the magistrates' court or the Crown Court, depending on the seriousness of the offence. The prosecutor will have to prove to the court, *beyond all reasonable doubt*, that the defendant committed the offence charged. The court will have to determine whether or not the defendant is guilty. In the magistrates' court it will usually be for the magistrates to determine this question, in the Crown Court it will be for the jury to decide questions of fact and for the judge to decide questions of law. A finding of *not guilty* will lead to the defendant's acquittal. A finding of *guilty* will lead to a conviction and may lead to a sentence of imprisonment or some other form of punishment such as a fine or probation.

One of the major objectives of the criminal law is to punish the wrongdoer for action that is deemed to be contrary to the interests of the state and its citizens. Criminal proceedings do not have as a major objective the provision of compensation or support for the victim of crime. It is significant that the exercise of the discretion to prosecute is seldom carried out by the victim of the crime. Criminal proceedings are normally initiated by the state or its agents and brought in the name of the Queen or the prosecuting official.

In civil proceedings it is generally the *claimant* (the party harmed) (before April 1999 known as the *plaintiff*) who sues the *defendant*, although in some areas of the civil law other terms are used. For example, in the case of a divorce the petitioner and a respondent. The case will usually be heard in either the County Court or the High Court, depending on the nature of the case and the size of the loss involved. The plaintiff usually has to prove, on *the balance of probabilities*, that the events took place in the manner claimed. This is a lower standard of proof than in criminal cases. If the plaintiff proves their case, the court will make some kind of order. What this will be will depend upon the kind of case and what the plaintiff has asked for. The basic choice before the court is whether to order the defendant to compensate the plaintiff for their loss by awarding damages or to order the defendant to act, or refrain from acting, in some specific way in the future, or to make both kinds of orders.

Historically the civil law was primarily founded on the law of contract and tort, which are still mainly areas of common law. The law of contract determines which forms of agreement entered into between individuals are legally binding and on whom they will be binding. The law of tort covers categories of civil wrong, other than breach of contract, which may give rise to legal causes of action. It includes the law of negligence, trespass and libel and slander. Just as a set of facts can give rise to conduct that may result in both civil and criminal proceedings, so a set of facts can give rise to both actions in contract and in tort. Most claimants' primary motivation for bringing civil proceedings will be to obtain an effective remedy for the civil wrong which has been perpetrated. The fact that there is liability will not, however, necessarily mean that they will take action. For example, there may be little point in suing a person for damages if you know they have no money.

In the latter part of the twentieth century areas of civil law other than those related to contract and tort came to be of increasing importance. Some took a very different form to contract and tort. Divorce, for example, necessitates an action in court but, unlike actions in contract and tort, such cases are rarely contested, although there may be separate court cases about what happens to either any children the divorcing couples may have or the property and income that they have. One area of law that is very important in the higher courts is public law. Public law is the law that governs those that are given powers by statute. These are largely bodies or individuals which form part of either central or local government. There is a more detailed explanation of the nature of public law in the final section of this chapter.

The emphasis of the civil law has changed over the last hundred years with an increase in the role of the state and the importance of legislation as opposed to case law as the major source of law. Civil law does not just regulate relations between individuals covering such matters as their property transactions, but also deals with relations between the state and individuals. It covers unemployment and social benefit entitlement, tax and planning questions, and council tenants' relationships with their local authorities. All of these areas are covered by statute law that has created new rights and obligations. These are often enforced in tribunals as opposed to courts.

Statutory provisions have also been enacted in order to change the common law rights that have resulted from the judicial development of contract law and the notion of freedom of contract. For example, employment protection and landlord and tenant legislation give employees and tenants statutory rights that will often modify or override terms in their contracts that give their employers or landlords specific rights to dismiss or evict them.

NATIONAL, INTERNATIONAL AND EUROPEAN UNION LAW

2.3 ▶ The term *national, municipal* or *state law* is used when referring to the internal legal rules of a particular country. In contrast *international law*, usually termed *public international law*, deals with the law that applies to external relationships of a state with other states. In the UK, national law is normally unaffected by international legal obligations unless these obligations have been put into national law by an Act of Parliament. *European Union law*, however, cuts across this conventional notion that national and international law operate at different and distinct levels. It is a form of international law in that it is in part concerned with legal relations between Member States, but EU law may also directly affect the national law of Member States. It will therefore be considered separately from both national and international law.

NATIONAL LAW

2.4 ▶ The system of national law has already been considered in Chapter 1.

INTERNATIONAL LAW

2.5 ▶ Public international law regulates the external relations of states with one another. (*Private international law* is a type of national law that deals with cases where individuals find themselves in legal disputes that involve a number of different countries; for example when someone from the UK makes a contract in France). Public international law, but not private international law, is a form of law that is very different from national law. There is no world government or legislature issuing and enforcing laws to which all nations are subject. The international legal order is essentially decentralised and operates by agreement between states. This means that the creation, interpretation and enforcement of international law lies primarily in the hands of states themselves. Its scope and effectiveness depends on the capacity of states to agree and the sense of mutual benefit and obligation involved in adhering to the rules.

International law is created in two main ways: by treaty and by custom. Treaties are agreements between two or more states, and are binding, in international law, on the states involved if they have given their consent to be so bound. Customary law is established by showing that states have adopted broadly consistent practices towards a particular matter and that they have acted in this way out of a sense of legal obligation. International law is neither comprehensive nor systematic. Few treaties involve the majority of world states. Most are bilateral understandings or involve only a handful of parties to a multilateral agreement.

Disputes about the scope and interpretation of international law are rarely resolved by the use of international courts or binding arbitration procedures of an international organisation. This is because submission to an international court or similar process is entirely voluntary and few states are likely to agree to this if there is a serious risk of losing their case or where important political or national interests are at stake. Negotiation is far more common. International courts are used occasionally, for example where settlement is urgent, or protracted negotiations have failed, where the dispute is minor or is affecting other international relations; in other words, in cases where failure to settle is more damaging than an unfavourable outcome. Where international law has been breached, an injured state must rely primarily on self-help for enforcement. There is no effective international institutional machinery to ensure compliance when the law is challenged. This means that in practice powerful states are better able to protect their rights and assert new claims.

Breaching established rules is one, rather clumsy, way of changing international law. In a decentralised system, change can only be effected by common consent or by the assertion of a new claim being met by inaction or acquiescence by others. The lack of powerful enforcement machinery does not mean that international law is widely disregarded. On the contrary, legal rules are regularly followed, not least because states require security and predictability in the conduct of normal everyday inter-state relations.

International law also plays an important role in the promotion of common interests such as controlling pollution, restricting over-fishing, or establishing satellite and telecommunication link-ups.

A large number of global or regional international organisations have been established for the regulation and review of current inter-state activity. The best-known example, though perhaps not the most effective, is the United Nations, whose primary function is the maintenance of international peace and security.

In the UK, international law has no direct effect on national law and, on a given matter, national law may in fact be inconsistent with the United Kingdom's international obligations. The Government has authority to enter into treaties which may bind the UK vis-à-vis other states. However a treaty will not alter the law to be applied within the UK unless the provisions are adopted by means of an Act of Parliament. Customary international law may have been incorporated into national law but will enjoy no higher status than any other provision of national law and is, therefore, liable to be superseded by a new statute. However, it is a principle of judicial interpretation that, unless there is clear legal authority to the contrary, Parliament does not intend to act in breach of international law. In some other countries, international law is accorded a different status. In the Netherlands and Germany, for example, international law takes effect in municipal law and, where these conflict, international law prevails.

The lack of direct application should not be taken to mean that international law is of no importance in UK courts or for UK citizens. National courts regularly decide domestic cases having presumed the existence and application of international law. For example, under the Vienna Convention of 1961, diplomats enjoy immunity from criminal prosecution. If a defendant claims immunity, a court must decide whether the defendant falls within the terms of the treaty before proceeding further. Secondly, individuals may have rights under international law, enforceable not through national courts but through international institutions. The European Convention on Human Rights gives individuals the right to complain of breaches of the Convention to the European Commission on Human Rights which may then refer the case to the European Court of Human Rights (these institutions should not be confused with European Union institutions: they are quite separate). Although the UK ratified the Convention in 1951, it was only in 1966 that the UK agreed to the articles of the treaty that recognised the right of individual petition and the compulsory jurisdiction of the Court. The Human Rights Act 1998 now gives an individual the right to enforce certain rights found in the Convention against public authorities.

EUROPEAN UNION LAW

▶ 2.6

In joining the European Communities in 1973, the UK agreed to apply and be bound by Community law, accepting that Community law would override any conflicting provisions of national law. Unlike other forms of international law, European Community law is capable of passing directly into national law; it is applicable in the UK without being adopted by an Act of Parliament. These principles were given legal effect by the passage of the European Communities Act 1972. The European Communities are made up of three organisations: the European Economic Community

(EEC), the European Coal and Steel Community (ECSC) and the European Community for Atomic Energy (Euratom). Since the UK's entry the European Communities have been further enlarged. There are now 28 member states. The European Communities are now part of the European Union, following the Treaty on European Union, signed at Maastricht (since added to by the Treaty of Amsterdam, Treaty of Nice and Treaty of Lisbon). This section will concentrate on the implications of membership of the European Union for United Kingdom law.

The European Union is an international organisation established and developed by treaty between Member States. The basic framework is set out in the EEC Treaty of 1957 (the Treaty of Rome), which defines the objectives of the Community, the powers and duties of Community institutions, and the rights and obligations of Member States. This treaty goes much further than just creating law that binds both Member States and Community institutions. It contains many detailed substantive provisions, some of which create rights for individuals that are enforceable directly in national courts. The EEC Treaty, and certain others which have followed it, are thus primary sources of European Union law. The European Union has a number of major institutions: the Council of the European Union, the Commission, the Assembly (or European Parliament), the Court of Justice (and the Court of First Instance) and the Court of Auditors. The terms of the various treaties give the European Union a powerful legislative, administrative and judicial machinery. The Treaty provides that further legislation may be made by the Council of Ministers and the Commission. This is called secondary legislation and takes three forms.

Regulations, once made, pass into the law of a Member State automatically. Regulations are *directly applicable*, that means that Member States do not have to take any action (such as passing an Act of Parliament) to implement them or to incorporate them into national law. Regulations are intended to be applied uniformly throughout the Community, and override any conflicting provisions in national law.

Directives are binding on Member States as to the result to be achieved, but leave each Member State with a choice about the method used to achieve that result. Member States are given a transitional period in which to implement the directive. This may involve passing a new law, making new administrative arrangements, or, where national law already conforms with the directive, taking no action. The Commission can initiate proceedings against a Member State if it believes the steps taken do not achieve the desired result. Although directives are addressed to Member States, in some circumstances an individual may be able to rely directly on certain parts, whether or not the Member State has taken implementing action. This is when the relevant part lays down an unconditional obligation and grants enforceable individual rights.

Decisions can be addressed to Member States, individuals or companies. They are binding only on the person to whom they are addressed and take effect on notification.

EU law is applied in Member States by their individual system of national courts and tribunals. When a point of EU law is crucial to a court's decision, the court may refer the case to the Court of Justice for a preliminary ruling on the interpretation of the point in question. Courts against whose decision there is no appeal (e.g. the Supreme Court) must make a reference to the Court of Justice when the case hinges on EU law unless the Court has already ruled on that particular issue. Once the Court of Justice has given a preliminary ruling, the case is referred back to the national court from which it originated, which must then decide the case. The Court of Justice will only answer questions put to it about the interpretation of EU law; it will not rule on national law or on conflict between national and EU law or apply its interpretation to the facts of the case. These are all matters for national courts. The Commission may bring an action in the Court of Justice against a Member State for breach of an obligation, such as the non-implementation of a directive. Proceedings may be taken against the Commission or the Council for failing to act where the EEC Treaty imposes a duty to act. There are also provisions for annulling legislation adopted by the Commission or Council, for example, where the action has exceeded the powers laid down by treaty.

At the time of writing the UK government has said that it intends to withdraw from the European Union. If it does this what the legal relations will be between the European Union and the UK is unclear.

PUBLIC AND PRIVATE LAW

Another distinction that may be drawn between different types of law is the division between *public law* and *private law*. Public law is largely concerned with the distribution and exercise of power by the state and the legal relations between the state and the individual. For example, the rules governing the powers and duties of local authorities, the operation of the NHS, the regulation of building standards, the issuing of passports and the compulsory purchase of land to build a motorway all fall within the ambit of public law. In contrast, private law is concerned with the legal relationships between individuals, such as the liability of employers towards their employees for injuries sustained at work, consumers' rights against shopkeepers and manufacturers over faulty goods, or owners' rights to prevent others walking across their land.

▶ **2.7**

The significance of the public/private law distinction operates at two levels. First, it is a very useful general classification through which we can highlight some broad differences, such as those in the purpose of law, in sources and forms of legal rules, and in remedies and enforcement. This is the way the idea of public/private law will be discussed here. However, the distinction is also used in a second, narrower sense; as a way of defining the procedure by which claims can be raised in court.

One way of thinking about a legal rule is to consider its purpose. The primary purpose underlying most private law rules is the protection of individual interests, whereas the aim of most public law provisions is the promotion of social objectives and the protection of collective rather than individual interests. The methods used to achieve these purposes also differ. A characteristic feature of public law is the creation of a public body with special powers of investigation, decision-making and/or enforcement in relation to a particular problem, whereas private law achieves its ends by giving individuals the right to take action in defence of their interests.

Many problems are addressed by both public and private law. Sometimes a single statute may include both private rights and liabilities alongside public law provisions.

Example

Ann lives next door to an industrial workshop run by Brenda. The machinery is very noisy and the process discharges fumes that make Ann feel ill. This sort of problem is tackled by both public and private law in a number of different ways.

(i) *As a neighbour, Ann may bring a private law action in nuisance, which is a claim that Brenda's activities unreasonably interfere with the use of Ann's land. Ann could claim compensation for the harm she has suffered and could seek an injunction to stop the harmful process continuing*

(ii)   There are also public law rules that may be invoked whether or not an. individual has or may be harmed, aimed at preventing the problem arising in the first place or controlling the situation for the public benefit. For example, when Brenda first started her workshop she would have needed to get planning permission from the local authority if her activities constituted a change in the use of the land. Planning legislation thus gives the local authority an opportunity to prevent industrial development in residential areas by refusing planning permission, or control it by laying down conditions. Other legislation gives the local authority powers to monitor and control various kinds of pollution and nuisances in their area, including noise and dangerous fumes. A further complex set of private rights and public regulations govern the working conditions of the workshop employees, who would also be affected by the noise and smells.

Public and private law also show differences in their origins and form. Some of the most important principles of private law are of ancient origin and were developed through the common law as individuals took their private disputes to court and demanded a remedy. The rules of private rights in contract, over land and inheritance, to compensation for physical injury or damage to property or reputation, were all first fashioned by judges in the course of deciding cases brought before them. In contrast, most public law rules are of comparatively recent origin and concern the use of statutory powers.

An important function of public law has its roots in constitutional theory. The actions of public bodies are only lawful if there is a legal rule granting the body authority to act in a given situation. A private individual needs no legal authority merely to act. It is assumed that a person acts lawfully unless there is a legal rule prohibiting that behaviour. Public law therefore has a facilitative function, for which there is no equivalent in private law, permitting a public body to take action that would otherwise be unlawful.

A feature of much recent public law is a shift towards the grant of broad discretionary powers to public bodies. This means that the same legislative framework can be used more flexibly, accommodating changes in public policy as to the purposes to which the powers should be put or the criteria for the exercise of these powers. This characteristic form of modern public law contrasts quite sharply with the relatively specific rights and duties to be found in private law, and in turn affects the way public and private law can be enforced. All private law is enforced by granting individuals the right to take action in defence of a recognised personal interest. For example, a householder may make a contract with a builder over the repair of a roof, and may sue the builder if the work or materials are of a lower standard than was specified in the contract. Not all public law can be enforced by way of individual action.

The enforcement of public law can be viewed from two perspectives. First, public law can be enforced when an official ensures that individuals or companies comply with standards set in statutes or delegated legislation, e.g. Environmental Health Officers making orders in relation to or prosecuting restaurants. Secondly, the enforcement of public law can also be seen as the matter of ensuring public authorities themselves carry out their duties and do not exceed their legal powers. Here, the form of public law statutes, mentioned above, rarely ties a public body to supplying a particular standard of service, as a contract may tie a builder, but gives a wide choice of lawful behaviour.

Even where legislation lays a duty on a public authority, there may be no corresponding right of individual action. For example, under the Education Act 1996, local education authorities are under a duty to ensure that there are sufficient schools, in numbers, character and equipment, for providing educational opportunities for all pupils in their area. However, nobody can sue the authority if the schools are overcrowded or badly equipped. The only remedy is to complain to the Secretary of State, who can make orders if satisfied that the authority is in default of their duties. The mechanism for controlling standards of public bodies is generally by way of political account-ability to the electorate or ministers rather than the legal process.

Some parts of public law do create individual rights and permit individual enforcement. In social security legislation, for example, qualified claimants have a right to certain benefits and may appeal against decisions on benefit to a tribunal. There is a procedure, special to public law, called *judicial review of administrative action* (usually referred to simply as *judicial review*), whereby an individual may go to the High Court alleging unlawful behaviour on the part of a public body. However, in order to go to court, the individual must show *sufficient interest* in the issue in question (this being legally defined) and the court has a discretion whether to hear the case or grant a remedy. This is quite different from proceedings in private law, where a plaintiff does not need the court's permission for the case to be heard but has a right to a hearing if a recognised cause of action is asserted and also a right to a remedy of some kind if successful.

CRIMINAL LAW AND CIVIL LAW ANSWERS

Legal consequences in questions 1–4:   ▶ 2.8

1. Norman's actions may give rise to both criminal and civil proceedings. He may be prosecuted for drink driving and related road traffic offences and, if convicted, will have a criminal record. He may also be sued by the woman or child who would wish to recover damages for the personal injuries they have suffered. Such an action would be a civil action. The same set of facts may give rise to both criminal and civil liability.
2. The use of some drugs is prohibited by law. Legislative changes from time to time alter both which drugs are prohibited and the punishment that follows from conviction.
3. Sue has committed no criminal offence. Neither the unborn child nor Chris, if it is Chris' child, have any right of civil action for any harm they may consider Sue has done to them. If Sue is not married to Chris her affair with Richard does not give rise to any possible legal action.
4. Robert has not committed any criminal offence. He is in no different a position in law to the person who has no money. Usha will be able to commence civil proceedings against him. She will be able to sue him for breach of contract. Robert's wealth makes it more likely that Usha will consider it worth suing him as she is more likely to be able to recover any damages. However she will also have to remember that Robert will, if he wishes, be able to hire the best lawyers so as to delay Usha's inevitable court victory.

▶ 3
Law and its Social Context

INTRODUCTION

3.1 ▶ This chapter is about the different kinds of questions that arise when studying law and the different techniques you need when studying them.

You might think that studying law is purely a matter of learning a large number of legal rules. If this were the case only one kind of question would ever arise, what is the content of any particular legal rule? However, simply learning a large number of legal rules is not a very useful way of learning about law. Learning the rules is like memorising the answers to a set of sums. It is of no help when the sums change. If all you do is learn a set of legal rules, when the rules change, when the law is altered, you are back where you started. At the very least, to use your legal knowledge, you also need to know how to find legal rules and how to find out if they have been changed. Thus, to the question "what is the content of the legal rule?" are added questions about how to find them. More importantly all legal scholars would agree that legal rules are sometimes not clear. The content of such rules, and some scholars would argue that most legal rules are like this, is the subject of debate. If you are studying law you therefore need to know not just what the legal rules are but how you argue about what the content of legal rules might be.

Not everyone interested in law is interested in questions about the content of legal rules. For example, we might ask whether it is ever right to disobey the law. Here we are concerned not simply with what the rule is but what we ought to do because of that rule. This is a question of ethics that might, in part, relate to the content of a legal rule but is much more about the nature of moral judgement. We need to decide what we should do but we also need to learn how to construct arguments that will convince others that we are right about what we do.

Legal rules are intended to change behaviour; they should have an impact on society. However knowing what a legal rule is does not tell us whether the rule is in fact being obeyed. Equally knowing what a legal rule is does not tell us whether the impact that it is having, even if it is being obeyed, is that which was intended. Scholars have long observed that there is a difference between *the law in books*, legal rules, and *the law in action*, what happens in practice once a legal rule has been created. This is so even if we are just concerned with what happens in the courts. The hierarchical nature of the courts means that the lower courts should obey the rulings in the higher courts but research has shown that this is not always the case. Whether we are concerned with looking at what the law is for an individual client or what influence the law has on society knowing what the legal rules are is not enough. We need to know what happens in practice.

The distinction between the law in action and the law in books is both easy to see and useful to use but it also has its limitations. Some questions about law seem to fit into neither category. For example, is our earlier question about disobedience to law a question about the law in action or the law in books? Information about what actually happens in the legal system will only tell us what people do, not whether their action is morally correct. Equally, being told what the legal rule says is of little help in helping us assess whether we are correct to obey it or not. The question does not appear to fall into either category.

The distinction between the law in action and the law in books is broad but crude. More sophisticated categories provide narrower, more precise distinctions. Thus questions about the nature of law that can include whether or not one has a duty to obey it can be grouped together under the title the philosophy of law or *jurisprudence*. Such categories are not firmly fixed and may be defined by different people in different ways. Thus some people would use the term the *sociology of law* to refer to all questions about the operation of the legal system in practice. Others would distinguish between questions about the relationship between law and other social forces and questions about how effective a legal rule is. They would see the first kind of question as falling within the sociology of law and the second as coming under the heading *socio-legal studies*. It is more important to be able to identify the different kinds of questions than give them the labels.

DIFFERENT QUESTIONS MEAN DIFFERENT ANSWERS

Knowing that there are different kinds of questions asked when studying law is of intellectual interest but does it have any further significance? What happens if you fail properly to identify the kind of question that you are asking? We can answer these questions by looking at one way in which different kinds of questions are commonly confused. ▶ 3.2

For many years it was assumed that legal rules that laid down what should happen were an accurate guide to what actually happened. The law in action was thought to correspond more or less exactly with the law in books. It was accepted that there were divergences but these were thought to be on a small scale and of no importance. However, academics have now shown that there is often a very great difference between legal rules and the practice in the legal system. One example of this can be seen in the area of criminal justice, when people are arrested and taken to the police station for questioning.

The Police and Criminal Evidence Act 1984 (generally referred to as "PACE") lays down a large number of rules relating to the treatment of suspects who are detained in police stations. The purpose of these rules is to try and provide a balance between providing safeguards for the person who is being questioned and enabling the police to carry out a thorough investigation. One of the rules that PACE contains is that the suspect must be told of his/her right to seek legal advice. However, researchers have found that most people do not receive legal advice at the police station. This can happen because many suspects do not appreciate how important it is to have legal advice at an early stage in criminal investigations. However, another significant reason influencing suspects in their decision not to seek legal advice is that the police may use a number of ploys to discourage suspects from taking advice, including minimising the significance of what is happening by saying the suspect will only be there for a short time, or emphasising what a long time the detainee will have to wait until their legal adviser arrives. Merely looking at the law in the books could only tell us what is supposed to happen; that suspects are entitled to be told about their right to seek legal advice. It is only when we look at the law in action that we can understand how the law really works in practice; in this case, we come to understand that merely giving a right to people does not mean that they will understand how important it is to exercise that right, nor does giving a right ensure that it will necessarily be implemented in the way it was intended.

The difference between the law in action and the law in books in this area is important for several reasons. First, confusing the different kinds of questions resulted in an inaccurate description. People accepted the wrong kind of material as evidence for their answers, and as a result thought that the law worked in practice in much the same way as the legal rules suggested it should. Secondly, because of that mistake, those involved in advising others on the law may have given misleading advice. Finally, those involved in considering whether or not the law and legal system are effective and just looked not at the real legal system but, instead, at a shadowy reflection of it.

WHICH KIND OF QUESTION AM I ASKING?

3.3 Somebody has been divorced and you are asked how their financial affairs will be settled by the courts. Are you being asked what the relevant rules are, or what will actually happen in court, or both? Outside your course of study it may be very difficult to sort out what kind of question you are being asked. For study purposes the task will generally be simpler. The kind of question that you are being asked is likely to be indicated by the nature of your course as a whole. The title of your course may give you a clue. A course on "the sociology of law" is unlikely to be much concerned with questions about the content of legal rules. Some kinds of courses are more usually taught with one kind of question in mind than another. For example, courses on "land law" or the "law of contract" are more often concerned with the law in books than the law in action. These kinds of courses are sometimes termed *black-letter law* courses. Courses on Family Law often include a great deal of material that tells us about the law in action. This kind of course is often described as *socio-legal*.

Even when it is clear what kind of question your course is generally concerned with problems may still arise. It is not only important to know the kind of question that you are interested in. You must also be able to identify the kind of question that the author of a book or article that you are using is interested in. Are they trying only to analyse the legal rules, the cases and statutes in a particular area of law, or are they also interested in exploring how the law works in practice? If you know the type of answer they are trying to give you will be in a better position to judge the quality of their argument and, thus, the value of their work. Even when you have identified the kind of question an author is most interested in you will also have to be careful to see that other kinds of question are not introduced. For example, it is not uncommon to find a book largely devoted to discussion of the content of legal rules also including a few remarks on the value or justice of those rules. There is nothing wrong with this if the author realises that a different kind of question is being addressed and uses the appropriate material to answer it. Unfortunately this is not always so.

ARE THERE REALLY DIFFERENT QUESTIONS?

3.4 There are some people who would argue that it is misleading to distinguish between different questions in the way we have done above. Some would argue that all the distinctions drawn are wrong. Others would argue that only some of them are invalid. Are there really different questions? One argument that might be advanced is about the distinction between the law in action and the law in books. The Court of Appeal has laid down strict rules about when people accused of offences can receive a lesser sentence if they plead guilty (a practice known as *plea-bargaining*). Research in the past in this area suggested that these rules were not followed in practice. If we assume that the practice of all courts is not to follow these rules, and if this practice continued for many years, what would it mean to say that the legal rule was that which had been laid down by the Court of Appeal? People would only be affected by what happened in practice that would always be different from that which the legal rules said should happen. Could we really say that the legal rule had any significance? If the legal rule has no significance, then surely all we ought to study is what happens in practice, ignoring questions about the law in books?

Other more complicated forms of the above argument exist. Some people would argue that when a judge makes a decision that decision is sometimes influenced by the judge's social background, political views and education. The result of any case is therefore not solely determined by the neutral application of legal rules but by factors personal to the particular judge in the case. If this is so, then what kinds of questions will discussion about the content of legal rules answer? If we are to advise people how to act so as to win cases in court what we need to discuss is not, or not only, the content of legal rules but, rather, who the judges are and what their background is. If we want to find out what the law is we have to ask a whole series of questions other than those about ratios or statutes.

In a similar fashion not everyone accepts that questions about the morality of law and questions about the content of law are different. For some people, the very idea of an immoral law is a contradiction in terms. They think that all law must have an irreducible minimum positive moral content. Without that content the "law", in their view, is merely a collection of words that make a command which may be backed by the physical power of the state but do not have the authority of law. Such theories are termed *natural law* theories. Others argue that the questions about whether something is a legal rule or not and questions about the moral content of that rule are quite distinct. This is usually termed a *positivist* approach to law.

The authors of this book would accept that the distinctions drawn in the previous sections are open to question. The relationship between the different questions, if there are different questions, may be more complicated than the simple divisions above. However most books and most courses in law draw the kinds of distinction outlined. At this early stage in your study of law it will be enough if you understand what the distinctions are. Even if later you come to reject some or all of them, you will still find yourself reading material that is based upon them.

ANSWERING QUESTIONS

This chapter has drawn a distinction between three types of question; those concerned with the nature of law, those concerned with the content of legal rules and those which address the operation of law and legal system in practice. Each type of question has a technique appropriate for answering it.

▶ **3.5**

Questions about the nature of law are those that are most difficult to answer. The questions are basic ones, appearing to be very simple. For example, how is law different from other types of command? What is the difference between a gunman telling me to do something and the state, through law, telling me to do something? Are both simply applications of power or is there something fundamentally different between them? Neither the content of particular legal rules nor the operation of the law in practice provides any answer. Arguments in this area are abstract and philosophical. In advancing and judging such arguments it is necessary to see that all the terms are explained and that the argument is coherent. Arguments used here must also match the world they purport to explain. In practice these simple conditions are very difficult to meet.

The ultimate source for answers to questions about the law in books are the judgments and statutes that have already been discussed in Chapter 1. Only these sources will give you a definitive answer to any question you are asked. You are told how to find these materials in Chapter 4 and how to use them in Chapter 5. In some cases you may not have either the time or the resources to consult original materials. In such instance you can look at some of the various commentaries on the law. These vary in size, depth of coverage and price. Different commentaries serve different purposes. Some are student texts. Others are written for specific professions or occupations. Most cover only a limited area of law. However there are some general guides to the law and some encyclopaedias of law. The best encyclopaedia of general English law is *Halsbury's Laws of England*. This has a section on almost every area of law. Most good reference libraries will have a copy of this, and your library may also contain some of the other commentaries that are available. All commentaries try to explain legal rules. You should select one suitable to your interests. However, always remember that a commentary is one person's opinion about the law. It may be wrong. You can only be sure what the rule is if you consult the original cases and statutes.

Finding out how the law works in practice is frequently much more difficult than deciding what a legal rule means. It is easy to find opinions about how things work. Almost everybody who has contact with the law, even if only through reading about it in the newspapers, has an opinion on such questions. However, such opinions have little value. At best they are the experience of one person. That experience may be unusual or misinterpreted by that person. What we are trying to understand is how the legal system works. Anecdotes do not give us the answers that we seek. Thus, to answer this kind of question, we need to turn to the materials and techniques of the social scientist.

SEEING THE LAW IN ACTION

3.6 ▶ One starting point for looking at the law in action is looking at statistical information about the legal system. This is one way of moving from the merely anecdotal to the general. Information about the number of cases handled by a court shows in specific terms what the court's workload is. Changes from year to year may indicate some effects of changes in the law and practice. Statistics here can be used descriptively to provide a clearer picture than general phrases such as "some", "many" or "a few". Statistical tests can also establish that there is a relationship, often called a *correlation*, between different things. For example, the length of a sentence for theft may correlate with the value of the items stolen or the experience of the judge who heard the case. This means that the sentence will be longer if, for example, more items are stolen or the judge is more experienced. Statisticians have produced tests to show whether, given the number of examples you have, there is a strong correlation or not. Where this correlation fits with a theory (sometimes termed an *hypothesis*) it provides evidence tending to confirm the theory. Such confirmation is important; without it we have little to establish the effect that the law has, being forced to rely on personal knowledge of individual instances of its application and having to assume that these have general truth. Empirical study of the operation of law may reveal areas for improvement. It can also confirm that, measured by particular standards, the courts are working well.

If we want to use statistics where will we get them from? Government departments collect and publish a large number of statistical reports relating to their operations. Many of these are now available not only in hardcopy form but online via the web. Thus, for example, the Office for National Statistics' data can be seen at *https://www.ons.gov.uk/*. The work of all Government departments is relevant when looking at how the legal system works. Some departments are, however, particularly important in this respect. The Ministry of Justice is one of the largest Government departments and is responsible for the court system, prisons and the probation service. Its website is *https://www.gov.uk/government/organisations/ministry-of-justice*. The Home Office is responsible for things such as the police, immigration and anti-terrorism. Its website is *https://www.gov.uk/government/ organisations/home-office*. The Department for Education (http://www.education.gov.uk/) and the Department for Work and Pensions (*https://www.gov.uk/government/organisations/ department-for-work-pensions)* also provide useful information. A complete list of Government departments together with their websites is to be found at *https://www.gov.uk/*.

Most official statistics are collected from returns filed by local offices of the relevant departments. The content of these is determined by what the department needs to know about its activities and also by what Parliament has asked it to report on. Even minor changes in the collection of official statistics means that it is often impossible to make comparisons over a period of years. The information collected in one year is about something different from that in other years. Moreover, because of the way in which information is collected and the purpose of collecting it, these statistics can only answer a few of the questions about the way the law operates. For example, the judicial statistics list the number of cases brought each year in the County Court, broken down according to the type of claim. They provide little or no information about the applicants, the specific point of law relied on or whether the judgment was successfully enforced.

Official statistics, as a source of information, are limited. They provide information about things of importance to those who collected them. These are not necessarily the things that are important to the researcher. Government departments, the research councils and some private bodies sponsor research into specific areas of law. Small-scale research is often undertaken without sponsorship. Although this research may be based upon official statistics it may involve first collecting the necessary statistics and then deciding what they mean. The researchers must collect the data they need for each project. They have to design the study that is to select the methods they will use and choose the sample to ensure that they have all the information relevant to their chosen topic. There is a more detailed discussion of some of these issues in Chapter 8, "Reading Research Materials".

The collection of statistics is only one way of gathering information about law and the legal system. Statistics are useful for describing things like numbers of events but are poor for describing things like motivations. Collecting them is one form of *quantitative research*. If researchers want to find out more about the reasons why the law affects people in certain ways, or how it affects them, they will have to carry out different types of research. This may involve interviewing people or even directly observing what is happening in the area in which they are interested. This is known as *qualitative research*. When conducting qualitative research researchers must decide how they can carry out their research so as to ensure that the material they collect represents not just the particular people or bodies they have studied but is also an accurate reflection of the world as a whole.

Socio-legal research has enabled us to understand in a whole range of situations the way in which the law works in practice. It has revealed, for example, how the work of solicitors varies widely, depending on what kind of firm is being considered and why people frequently do not seek the legal redress that they are entitled to. Socio-legal research offers us the opportunity to extend our knowledge of the law and the legal system far beyond the boundaries of the law in the books, showing us how legal rules are affected by the political, economic and social contexts in which law operates.

Part 2

▶ 4
Finding cases and statutes

In Chapter 1 the importance of cases and statutes as sources of law was explained. This chapter explains how you find reports of cases and copies of statutes and how you make sure that they are up-to-date. As has been explained, these materials are primary sources of law. From them it is possible to derive the legal rules in which you are interested. Chapters 5, 6 and 7 will explain in more detail how this is done.

FINDING CASES

In the following, the task of discovering case reports will be considered for three different sets of circumstances:

▶ 4.2

    (a) Where a well-stocked and supported library is available.
    (b) Where some research or library facilities are available, but without access to a fully-equipped law library.
    (c) With the aid of online computerised retrieval facilities.

Most readers will have different facilities available at different times. For example, a reader who has access to a fully-equipped law library can only use it during opening hours. It is important that you are aware of the different ways in which to find cases so that you can decide which is the best method to use at any particular time.

USING FULL LAW LIBRARY NON-ELECTRONIC RESEARCH FACILITIES

The traditional form of research in relation to law reports is performed in law libraries containing a wide selection of materials and a variety of support systems, indexes, catalogues, etc. designed to assist the researcher in the task of locating and using particular items. Such libraries are found in academic institutions, such as universities, as well as in professional institutions such as the Inns of Court. In many cases, it is possible to use such libraries even if you are not a member of the institution. What follows in this chapter is an introduction to the major series of law reports and the basic methods of locating and checking up-to-date material and of updating earlier materials.

▶ 4.3

    Law reports go back over 700 years, although most of the case reports you will find in a normal law library have been decided during the last 150 years. Reports are divided into different series. The way in which these series are compiled varies. Sometimes the series are systematic in their coverage, reporting cases in a particular area of law or from a particular court. In other instances coverage is more general and even idiosyncratic. Older cases can be found in series which bear the title of the name (or names) of the law reporter(s). Such a series is the nineteenth century series of Barnewall and Alderson (Bar & Ald) (all law reports have abbreviations that are customarily used when discussing them. Whenever a series is first mentioned here its usual abbreviation will be given, in brackets, as above. Appendix II to this book is a list of useful abbreviations, including those to the main law reports). The only necessary coherence these cases have is that the reporter thought it was worthwhile to print them. The range and variety of these older cases is enormous, although some help has now been provided to modern legal researchers with some of the old series reprinted in a new collection under the title of *The English Reports* (E.R.). In 1865 the Incorporated Council of Law Reporting introduced *The Law Reports*, a series that was divided according to the different courts of the day. The Council has continued these reports though the current divisions of the reports are different. Today one can find the following divisions:

(a) Appeal Cases (A.C.)—reports of cases in the Court of Appeal, the House of Lords, the Supreme Court and the Privy Council.
(b) Chancery Division (Ch.)—report of cases in the Chancery Division of the High Court and cases appealed from there to the Court of Appeal.
(c) Queen's Bench (Q.B.)—reports of cases in the Queen's Bench Division of the High Court and cases appealed from there to the Court of Appeal.
(d) Family Division (Fam.)—reports of cases in the Family Division of the High Court and cases appealed from there to the Court of Appeal (until 1972 the Family Division was the Probate, Divorce and Admiralty Division (P.)).

This series is the closest to an "official" series of law reports. If a case is reported in several different series and there is a discrepancy between the different reports it is *The Law Reports* that should normally be followed. There is, nowadays, a wide range of privately-published law reports. Most of these series concentrate upon a particular area of legal developments, e.g. the law relating to industrial relations, or the law concerning road traffic. However, there are two series that publish cases dealing with decisions affecting a wide range of legal issues. These general series, with which most students of law will quickly become familiar, are the *Weekly Law Reports* (W.L.R.) and the *All England Law Reports* (All E.R.).

Each of the modern series, just discussed, reports fully any case contained in its volumes. Everything that the judge or judges said in judgment is to be found in the report. There are, in addition, some sources that provide a short summary of, or extracts from, judgments given. The most up-to-date of these sources are those newspapers that print law reports. *The Times* has contained such reports for the longest time and is regarded as being the most authoritative source of such reports. As well as being in The Times, they are now available online on a separate site (*https://www.justis.com/data-coverage/times-law-reports.aspx*). Case-note sections published in legal periodicals such as the *New Law Journal* (N.L.J.) or the *Solicitors' Journal* (S.J. or Sol. Jo.) are also a good source of such summaries. Where a full report of a case is available as well as short summaries or extracts it is the full report that should be considered. Extracts or summaries, where full reports are available, are not primary sources of law. They cannot be cited in court. They reflect what the editor of the report thinks are the important parts of a judgment. The judgment as a whole is law. The editor's opinion of the law is merely that, opinion. However such summaries or extracts can be used when there is no full judgment reported elsewhere and they are the only source available.

USING LAW REPORTS

Every case which is reported in a series of law reports can be referred to by way of the names of the ▶ **4.4**
parties concerned in the action. Thus, where a court action is brought by somebody called Harriman
in dispute with somebody called Martin, the case can be referred to as *Harriman v Martin*. However,
referring to a case in this way is of limited usefulness. The reference does not tell the reader the
date of the case nor does it indicate the series of reports in which it is found. It does not even tell us
to which case involving a Harriman and a Martin the reader is being referred. There may be several.
Thus, in addition to its name, each reported case possesses a unique reference indicator. This normally includes (although not always in the same order):

(1) a reference to the title of the series of law reports in which the report is to be found;
(2) a date (year) reference. Where the date reference is necessary if you are to find the case
the date is normally enclosed in square brackets. Some series have individual volume
numbers for each year. The date reference is then put in round brackets;
(3) a reference to the volume number (if there is more than one volume of the particular
law reports series in the year concerned);
(4) a reference to the page or paragraph number at which the report of the case may be located.

If the case of *Harriman v Martin* is reported in the first volume of the *Weekly Law Reports* for 1962, at
p.739, the reference would be [1962] 1 W.L.R. 739. This is sometimes called the citation for the case.
If you know this reference or citation, it is possible to go directly to the shelves of the law library
which house the volumes containing that reference and to turn directly to the report of the case.
    Increasingly people are turning to the web as a source of law reports. This has led to the crea-
tion of a system of *neutral citation* for such reports. Under this system, which first began in 2001
courts and tribunals have their own abbreviation and each case is given a unique official number
by the courts. Within judgements, each paragraph has its own number.

References for the Supreme Court look like this:
[2009] UKSC 1
References for the House of Lords look like this:
[2006] UKHL 20
References for the Privy Council look like this:
[2006] UKPC 4
References for the Court of Appeal look like this:

Court of Appeal (Civil)	[2003] EWCA Civ 1
Court of Appeal (Criminal)	[2003] EWCA Crim 1

References for the High Court look like this:

Chancery Division	[2003] EWHC 123 (Ch)
Patents Court	[2003] EWHC 124 (Pat)
Queen's Bench	[2003] EWHC 125 (QB)
Administrative Court	[2003] EWHC 126 (Admin)
Commercial Court	[2003] EWHC 127 (Comm)
Admiralty Court	[2003] EWHC 128 (Admlty)
Technology and Construction Court	[2003] EWHC 129 (TCC)
Family Division	[2003] EWHC 130 (Fam)

Where it is necessary to refer to a precise passage in a judgment by using a paragraph number the paragraph number is put in square brackets. Where a neutral citation is available it is put first before the more traditional citation to a printed hardcopy version of the judgment.

Some tribunals such as the Employment Appeal Tribunal and the Upper Tribunal also use a system of neutral citation when reporting their cases.

If you know only the names of the parties in the case, you will need first to search for the specific citation, whether it be a neutral citation or a more traditional reference to a printed volume. Although it would be possible to search the indexes for each individual series of law reports for the names of a case, this would be an inefficient and time-consuming approach. Normally, therefore, recourse is had to a general reference manual, which is known as a *case citator*. One example is the case citator published by *Current Law*. Other means are also available for locating the references of specific cases but *Current Law* is that which is most readily available. What follows is a brief description of the *Current Law Case Citator*. The *Current Law* system of citations for cases works through a combination of three separate reference items which were at the time of writing:

(1) four hardbound citators covering the periods 1947–1976, 1977–1997, 1998–2001 and 2002–2004;

(2) a laminated volume for each of the years from 2005 until 2015;

(3) "Monthly Parts", which are issued regularly in pamphlet form. These are subsequently replaced by a bound volume for the year.

The importance of using all three items to complement one another will appear when we consider the problem of locating up-to-date references (see below).

Entries in the *Current Law Case Citator* are listed by title of case, arranged alphabetically. Thus, to find the law reports reference to the case of *Harriman v Martin* you need to turn to the alphabetical heading under "Harriman".

This reads: *Harriman v Martin* [1962] 1 W.L.R. 739; 106 S.J. 507; [1962] 1 All E.R. 225 C.A. . .. Digested 61/1249: Referred to, 72/2355.

From this information, we discover not only the law report's reference to the first volume of the *Weekly Law Reports* for 1962, at page 739, but also that there are reports of the same case in:

106 S.J. 507, i.e. the 106th volume of the *Solicitors' Journal* at page 507 and: [1962] 1 All E.R. 225, i.e. the first volume of the *All England Reports* for 1962 at page 225.

We are also told that the court that delivered the decision reported at those locations was:

C.A., i.e. the Court of Appeal.

Next, we are told that a "digest" (a brief summary) of the case has been included in a companion volume to the *Current Law Case Citator* at:

62/1249, i.e. in the companion year volume of *Current Law* for 1962 at paragraph 1249.

Finally, we are told that the case was "referred to" (in another case) and that that case is to be found at:

72/2355, i.e. in the companion year volume of *Current Law* for 1972 at paragraph 2355.

It now only remains to locate one of these volumes in the law library, and to turn to the appropriate page for a report on the case of *Harriman v Martin*. The above is not only a method for finding the reference to a case. If you already have a reference to a case, but you find that volume already in use in the library, you can use the method above to find an alternative citation for the case.

UPDATING CASES

It is not enough to know merely what was said in a particular case in order to know the importance that should be attached to that case. It is also necessary to know whether such an earlier case has been used or referred to subsequently by the judges, or, indeed, whether it has been expressly approved or disapproved of by a later court. If a case is approved by a court that is further up the hierarchy of courts than the court originally giving judgment (and that approval is part of the ratio of that later case) then the case will take on the status of the later decision. Thus a decision of the High Court approved by the Court of Appeal will take on the status of the Court of Appeal. Even if the approval forms part of the obiter within the later judgment this will be significant, indicating the way in which the court is likely to give judgment once the matter becomes central in a decision at that level. Disapproval of a case will be important in a similar fashion. Such information can be discovered by using the *Current Law Case Citator*. We can regard a case as reliable (or, at least, not unreliable) where we are informed that it has been "referred to", "considered", "explained", "followed", "approved" or "applied". On the other hand, considerable care must be taken with a case that has been "distinguished" while cases that have been "disapproved" or "overruled" are unlikely to prove reliable for future purposes.

▶ 4.5

Example

1.   From the Current Law Case Citator for 1977–97

Fort Sterling Ltd v South Atlantic Cargo Shipping NVC (The Finrose) [1994] 1 Lloyd's Rep. 559 QBD. .. .. Digested 95/4504

This tells us the location of the report of the case as explained above. It also says that the case was decided in the QBD (i.e. the Queen's Bench Division) and we are told that there is a digest of the case in the Current Law Year Book for 1995 at paragraph 4504.

2.   From the Current Law Case Citator for 1998–2001

Fort Sterling Ltd v South Atlantic Cargo Shipping NVC (The Finrose) [1994] 1 Lloyd's Rep. 559, QBD. .. .. Digested 95/4504. Applied, 00/244; Considered 00/569.

This gives us both the information that we had before and also tells us that the case has been applied in another case and considered in yet another case. In both instances we are given the reference to the appropriate Current Law Year Book that will enable us to look these two new cases up. If we look up the 2000 Year Book we find that the case at paragraph 244 is Thyssen Inc v Calypso Shipping Corp SA [2000] 2 All ER (Comm) 97 David Steel J. QBD (Comm Ct).

This gives us the name of the case that applied Fort Sterling Ltd v South Atlantic Cargo Shipping NVC (The Finrose), a reference to the law report where we can find the case reported (note that All ER (Comm) mentioned here is a different series of law reports to the more common ALL ER that we have discussed elsewhere in this book), the name of the judge in the case and the court where it was heard, the Commercial Court in the Queen's Bench Division. The paragraph also gives a short description of the judgement. Looking up paragraph 569 gives us similar information about Bua International Ltd v Hai Hing Shipping Co Ltd.

Looking up the Case Citator for 2002 to 2004, the year volumes for 2005 to 2015 gives us no further reference to Fort Sterling Ltd v South Atlantic Cargo Shipping NVC (The Finrose) so we now have a complete history of the case.

USING LIMITED LIBRARY FACILITIES

4.6 The problems of finding and using cases and law reports where limited resources are available are significant. Clearly, it will not be possible to find reports of all the cases that you may need, since the available reports may only be found in series which are not at your disposal. By the same token, you may not have access to sufficiently comprehensive reference manuals, such as a case law citator or similar. You may have access to one of the general series of law reports. This will often be a set of *All England Law Reports*. Many public reference libraries possess a set of these law reports. If this is the case, some searching for cases can be done using the index contained in those volumes, though this will, of course, be time consuming. Alternatively, if you are concerned only with a limited specialist area you may have access to a specialised series of law reports. Whatever your source of available material, however, it is of paramount importance that you familiarise yourself with the specific indexing and cross-referencing system adopted by that source. If you do this, you will be able to use the material at your disposal, limited though it may be by comparison with the resources of a fully-equipped and supported law library, in the most efficient manner. It will also be important to discover whether you can obtain access to some means for updating the material contained in your available sources. The use of a citator, as explained above, is clearly of major benefit, for the consolidation of information within one reference item avoids the necessity of searching through a range of separate volumes and series. Amongst possible sources of updated information might be the general legal periodicals, such as the *New Law Journal* or the *Solicitors' Journal* (both of which have been referred to above). Many public libraries subscribe to one of these, or to other relevant periodicals. Where your needs relate to a specific area, the periodicals available in relation to that area may be of assistance in obtaining up-to-date information. Thus, for example, many human resource management journals contain information about cases decided by the courts in relation to employment law. All of these will probably refer you to sources of information that you do not have but they will also enable you to make the most efficient use of those sources that are available. A further common source of information will be textbooks on the subject about which you are seeking information. The important rule here is to check that you have access to the latest possible edition of the book, and to bear in mind the possibility that case law developments may have overtaken the legal position as it was stated at the time of writing of the book. Most books dealing with the law will contain a statement in the "Foreword" stating the date on which the information given in the book is said to be current. In some instances, you may have access to a casebook. This term is something of a misnomer since casebooks frequently contain not just cases but also statutes and comments on the law. Such books are generally concerned with a specific topic, for example "contract law", and contain edited material relevant to the area. These books can be a very useful source where you have access only to limited library facilities. However, they suffer from several deficiencies. First, the reader relies on the editor of the volume to select the most appropriate material. There is no way in which the quality of the work can be checked. Secondly, the material presented may only be given in part. Again, the reader must trust that the editor has not given misleading extracts. Finally, the reader has no means of updating the material. In some areas of law encyclopaedias are produced. These are similar to casebooks, although they are generally more detailed. Publishers of this kind of work often supply an updating service. Increasingly, encyclopaedias are produced in a looseleaf form and the reader will substitute new pages as supplements are issued.

USING ELECTRONIC RETRIEVAL FACILITIES

To complete this section on finding and using reports of cases, mention must be made of the important and fast-developing range of computerised information retrieval systems. ▶ **4.7**

"Online" Services

There are two major, commercially marketed, legal databases which are widely used in universities and by practitioners, LEXIS and WESTLAW. Both databases cover a number of different jurisdictions and contain not just cases but also legislation and law journals. To use either of these systems effectively requires some training in the way that material is organised and the methods used to search them. ▶ **4.8**

In general both LEXIS and WESTLAW contain the full text of judgements though the format is somewhat different to that in traditional printed law reports. As well as providing access to a large collection of published legal material LEXIS and WESTLAW also include unreported cases, i.e. cases that have been decided but which have not yet been published in hardcopy form and in some cases never will be published in that form.

Searching for a case using electronic retrieval systems is generally done using key words. The user asks whether a specific term or set of words is to be found in the database. The user is then given a list of the cases that contain the item that is being searched for and can then look at the cases that have been found. The user will find that on the one hand if they use only very general terms for their search they will be given a very large list of cases to look at, most of which they will find irrelevant to their needs. If on the other hand they use a very precise term the list provided will not contain any case that is relevant but which uses slightly different terminology in its judgment. The skill in using databases like LEXIS and WESTLAW lies in steering a course between these two extremes.

Databases such as LEXIS and WESTLAW are highly effective ways of finding cases, finding citations for cases and for seeing if a case has been referred to in any other judgment.

Cases on the net

There are many internet sites which discuss law or legal issues or provide material about law. A number of these provide free access to legal materials. ▶ **4.9**

A wide range of material relating to law is available on the British and Irish Legal Information Institute's web site:

http://www.bailii.org/

All decisions of the Supreme Court are available at:

https://www.supremecourt.uk/decided-cases/

Decisions of the House of Lords are available at:

http://www.publications.parliament.uk/pa/ld/ldjudgmt.htm Privy Council decisions are available at: *http://www.jcpc.uk/decided-cases/index.html*

FINDING AND UPDATING STATUTES

4.10 ▶ Statutes are published individually but law libraries and some public libraries have bound collections that include all the statutes for a particular year. Statutes passed since 1988 are available on the internet at:

http://www.legislation.gov.uk/ukpga

With statutes there are three main problems. Is the statute in force? Has the statute been repealed by Parliament, (i.e. replaced by some other statute)? Has the statute been amended by Parliament, (i.e. had part of its contents altered by Parliament)? Starting with a provision in an Act of Parliament it is necessary to use one of the "citator" systems in order to discover the most recent changes (if any) that have affected that provision. The following example shows how to update a relatively recent statutory provision using the *Current Law Legislation Citator.*

Example

Let us take the Children Act 1989 section 8(4). In its original form this provision was set out as follows:

Residence, contact and other orders with respect to children

   8   *(1). . .*

        (2). . .

        (3). . .

        (4) The enactments are-

            (a) Parts I, II and IV of this Act;

            (b) the Matrimonial Causes Act 1973;

            (c) the Domestic Violence and Matrimonial Proceedings Act 1976;

            (d) the Adoption Act 1976;

            (e) the Domestic Proceedings and Magistrates' Court Act 1978;

            (f) sections 1 and 9 of the Matrimonial Homes Act 1983;

            (g) Part III of the Matrimonial and Family Proceedings Act 1984.

If we assume that in January 2017 we want to discover whether there have been changes to the wording of section 8(4) it is first necessary to turn to the volume of the Current Law Legislation

Citator that covers the period following the enactment of the Children Act 1989. This is the volume for 1989–1995.

The Current Law Legislation Citator is arranged in chronological order by year and by Chapter number for each Act. Chapter numbers are fully explained at p.00. For the Children Act1989 this is Chapter 41. We now need to look for our provision, section 8(4). The entry gives us details of many cases but makes no reference to any amendments. Our search must be continued in later volumes.

In the Current Law Legislation Citator for 1996 to 1999 there are the following entries:

> *s.8, amended: 1996 c.27 Sch.8 para.41, Sch.8 para.60, 1998 c.37 s.119. Sch.8 para.68*
> *s.8, repealed (in part): 1996 c.27 Sch.10*

We now know that the section was amended by Schedule 8 of the statute whose reference is 1996 chapter 27 and also by the statute whose reference is 1998 chapter 37. It was also repealed in part by Schedule 10 of the statute whose reference is 1996 chapter 27.

We now need to continue our search beyond 1999 by checking the more recent volumes of the Current Law Legislation Citator for 2000 to 2001 and for 2002 to 2004 and then the subsequent year volumes. In the 2002 to 2004 volume there is an entry that reads: s.8, amended: 2002 c.38 Sch.3 para.55, 2004 c.33 Sch.27 para.129. After this we must turn to the individual year volumes. In the year volume for 2014 there is an entry for s. 8 which reads: s.8 amended: 2014 c. 16, s.12, Sch. 2 para.3.

There are no further references to section 8 in the remaining tear volume for 2015.

We can now look up the statutes that we have found and see what changes have been made to section 8(4).

HOW TO USE ENCYCLOPAEDIAS

Encyclopaedias are not a source of law (although they may contain sources of law). Cases and statutes are sources of law. They are what will be used when judges are deciding what the outcome of a case is to be. However, for some people encyclopaedias will be the only material they have available. Thus it is important to consider how they can be used most effectively. Different examples of encyclopaedias vary in form and content. They do not all contain the same kind of material nor are they ordered in the same way. Therefore it is not possible to give a series of rules saying how encyclopaedias should be used. What follows are points that a reader should consider when first using any encyclopaedia. The first thing to look at is the kind of material that the encyclopaedia contains. One advantage of an encyclopaedia can be that it brings together a wide variety of material about particular subject matter. Thus, you may find the encyclopaedia which you are reading contains all the statutes in a particular area, all the statutory instruments, government circulars and other non- statutory material, references to relevant cases (with some description of their contents) together with some discussion of the application of legal rules in the area. On the other hand the encyclopaedia may contain only some of the material or may extract some of it. Thus, for example, instead of having all of a statute you may find that you have only parts of it. Even if the encyclopaedia claims to be fully comprehensive, remember that it is no more than a claim. The editors of the encyclopaedia may feel that they have included all

▶ 4.11

relevant statutes; others may disagree with them. It is always as important to be aware of what you do not know as what you do know. Relying on an encyclopaedia means that there may be gaps in your knowledge of the particular area of law. However, you may feel it worth relying on the encyclopaedia because it is the only source available. Equally, you may find it quicker to use an encyclopaedia and consider the advantage of speedy access more important than any element of doubt in your knowledge of the area. Most encyclopaedias extract at least some of the material that they cover. That is to say that they contain extracts of a statute, statutory instrument, or whatever, rather than the whole. Here the problem is that, in extracting their material, the editors of the encyclopaedia limit your knowledge of the law. You rely on them to extract that which is relevant and cannot check the matter for yourself. As a source of law, the less comprehensive an encyclopaedia is the less useful it will be. However, the more comprehensive an encyclopaedia is the slower it may be to use. Before using the encyclopaedia you need to consider the kind of question that you are trying to answer. If the question is a very broad and general one about the framework of some area of law you may find an encyclopaedia with less detail easier to use. However, if you are trying to answer a very detailed point, perhaps applying the law to a very precise factual situation, you need the most comprehensive encyclopaedia that you can find. Most encyclopaedias, and increasingly many other books about law, are now issued in looseleaf form. This means that the publisher issues supplements to the encyclopaedia on a regular basis. These supplements, which contain descriptions of changes in the law, are then substituted for the pages that discuss the out-of-date law. The advantage of the looseleaf form over ordinary books is that it means the encyclopaedia is more likely to be accurate. When using looseleaf encyclopaedias before looking up the point of law that interests you always see when it was last updated. You will usually find a page at the front of the first volume of the encyclopaedia that tells you when it was last updated. The technique for finding out about points of law in an encyclopaedia will vary depending upon the encyclopaedia being used. Some are organised according to different areas of law within the subject of the encyclopaedia. Others have different volumes for different kinds of material; one volume for statutes, one for discussion of the law and so forth. Most will have both indexes and detailed contents pages. Most encyclopaedias have a discussion of how they should be used at the beginning of their first volume. Always consult this when first using an encyclopaedia.

FINDING AND USING MATERIAL ON THE LAW OF THE EUROPEAN COMMUNITIES, THE EUROPEAN UNION, AND THE EUROPEAN ECONOMIC AREA

4.12 ▶ All basic material in relation to the European Communities, the European Union, and the European Economic Area is published in English. However, some material is not made available in all of the official languages of the European Communities immediately. What is said here refers specifically to English language versions of such material.

The Official Journal of the European Communities is the authoritative voice of the European Communities, and is used to publish daily information. It can be found at *http://eur-lex.europa.eu/oj/direct-access.html*. The *Official Journal* (the O.J.) is divided into two major parts (the L and C series). There are also separately published notices of recruitment, notices and public contracts and the like, which are published in a Supplement and in Annexes. Twice a year the O.J. issues a Directory of Community legislation in force and other acts of the Community institutions.

LEGISLATION

The L series (Legislation) contains the text of Community legislation. The series is arranged by Volume, starting in 1958, and by issue number sequentially throughout the issue year. Thus, the text of Council Directive 95/45/EC of 22 September 1994 on the establishment of a European Works Council or a procedure in Community-scale undertakings and Community-scale groups of undertakings for the purposes of informing and consulting employees is to be found in the *Official Journal* of September 30, 1994.

▶ **4.13**

> The Volume number for 1994 is Volume 37
> The issue number of the OJ L series for September 30, 1994 is L 254
> The text of the Directive is set out on page 64 and thus the page reference is p.64
> The official reference for the Directive will be OJ No L 254, 30.9.1994, p.64

INFORMATION AND NOTICES

The C series (Information and Notices) contains, amongst a host of other items, key extracts (*the operative part*) from judgments of the Court of Justice of the European Communities (the ECJ, sitting in Luxembourg) and the Court of First Instance (which also sits in Luxembourg). Where the language of the particular court being reported is not English, the C series will include *a provisional translation*: the definitive translation being found in the separately published Reports of Cases before the Court. There is also brief coverage of actions brought before the ECJ by Member States against the Council of the European Communities, as well as questions referred to the ECJ by national courts of Member States. Also, to be found in the C series will be Preparatory Acts in the course of being made into legislation by the European Communities. Thus, for example, the *Official Journal* for February 19, 1994 contains the text of an Opinion delivered by the Economic and Social Committee on a proposal for a Council Regulation on substances that deplete the ozone layer.

▶ **4.14**

> The Volume Number for 1994 is Volume 37
> The issue of the OJ C series for 19 February 1994 is C 52
> The text of the proposed Decision is item 3 in issue C 52, and so the reference is 03
> The full reference for the Opinion is OJ 94/C 52/03.

OTHER MATERIALS

Whilst the *Official Journal* is the best official source of information about Community law it should be noted that a wide range of documentation does not find its way into the *Official Journal* and other sources may have to be considered for those wanting a comprehensive list of European materials. In particular, mention should be made of so-called COM documents, which often contain important proposals for future legislation. These are issued by the Commission with a "rolling" numerical reference by sequence of publication during a particular year. Consequently, there is no systematic numbering of such COM Docs a matter which frequently gives rise to criticism about the accessibility of important documentation in the legislative field. By way of example, an important Communication concerning the application of the Agreement on social policy, presented by the Commission to the Council and to the European Parliament on 14 December 1993, is simply designated:

▶ **4.15**

COM(93) 600 final

Various other series, apart from the COM series, are also to be found in relation to a range of spheres of activity within the European Union. Judgments of the European Court of Justice are reported in two series of law reports. One series is that formally published by the European Union itself the *European Court Reports* (E.C.R.). The other series is the privately produced *Common Market Law Reports* (C.M.L.R.). Both can be found in the normal manner. In addition to these specialised law reports series, an increasing number of judgments delivered by the European Court of Justice are now reported as a normal part of general law report series.

EUROPEAN UNION MATERIALS ON THE INTERNET

4.16 ▶ The official internet site of the European Union is found at: *http://europa.eu* From here it is possible to access all the institutions of the European Union in any of the official languages of the Union.

▶ 5
Reading cases and statutes

This chapter will explain how you should use the primary sources for legal rules, cases and statutes. You will find a specimen case report and a specimen statute in each section. In addition, there are further examples of case reports in the exercise section of this book (Cases I and II). Skill in the use of the techniques described here can only be acquired with practice. For this reason the exercises in the book enable you to build a range of experience in handling the material contained in cases and statutes.

▶ 5.1

READING A CASE

The contents of law reports are explained here so that you can start to read cases, understand the law which they contain, and make useful notes about them. You will find the court structure, and how cases are decided, explained in Chapter 1. You will find a copy of a case, *R. v Jackson*, on pp.40–42. All specific references in this section will be to that case. The copy is taken from the *All England Law Reports*, which are the most commonly available law reports. However, if you have access to other kinds of hard copy law reports you will find that they look very much the same as the *All England Law Reports*. The techniques discussed here will be just as useful in reading other series of law reports and court transcripts. The different series of law reports and their use has been explained in Chapter 4.

▶ 5.2

R v Jackson

a

COURT OF APPEAL CRIMINAL DIVISION
ROSE L.J., BUTTERFIELD AND RICHARDS JJ
28 APRIL, 1998

Criminal law—Appeal—Leave to appeal—Practice—Single judge granting leave on *b*
some grounds but refusing leave on others—Need for leave of full court to pursue
grounds in respect of which leave refused.

Where, on an application for leave to appeal to the Court of Appeal, Criminal
Division, the single judge grants leave on some grounds but specifically refuses leave
on others, counsel for the appellant must obtain the leave of the full court if he *c*
wishes to pursue the grounds in respect of which leave has been refused (see
p. 574g. post).

Notes
For appeal against conviction or sentence following trial on indictment, see 11(2)
Halsbury's Laws (4th edn reissue) paras 1352, 1355. *d*

Cases referred to in judgment
R v Bloomfield [1997] 1 Cr App R 135, CA.
R v Chalkley, R v Jeffries [1998] 2 All ER 155, [1998] QB 848, [19983] WLR 146, CA.

e

Appeal against conviction
Stephen Shaun Jackson appealed with leave of the single judge against his
conviction on 25 July 1995 in the Crown Court at Croydon before Judge Crush
and a jury of theft. The facts are set out in the judgment of the court.

Marc Willers (assigned by the *Registrar of Criminal Appeals*) for the appellant. *f*
Hugh Davies (instructed by the *Crown Prosecution Service*, Croydon) for the Crown.

ROSE LJ delivered the following judgment of the court. On 25 July 1997 in the
Crown Court at Croydon, this appellant was convicted by the jury of theft, on the
first count in the indictment. He was acquitted of charges of false accounting on
counts 2, 3 and 4. The trial was a retrial, the jury on an earlier occasion having *g*
acquitted in relation to certain counts on the then indictment, but failed to agree
in relation to the counts upon which the second jury adjudicated. He appeals
against his conviction by leave of the single judge, which was granted in relation
to the first of the two matters which Mr Willers, on behalf of the appellant, seeks
to canvass before this court. *h*
    For the purposes of this appeal, the facts can be briefly stated. The appellant
was the proprietor of a minicab firm. Insurance brokers, Thompson Heath &
Bond (South East) Ltd (to whom we shall refer as 'THB') devised a scheme to
enable minicab drivers to pay for their motor insurance by instalments. That
scheme was underwritten by others. *j*
    The scheme allowed the premiums to be collected from the minicab drivers on
a weekly basis, and passed on to THB each month. THB then paid the
underwriters.
    It was the Crown's case against the appellant that, while he acted as agent for
THB, to collect weekly premiums from the drivers, between February 1991 and
March 1994, he failed to declare to THB the full amount that he had collected,

a and that he kept a sum of money, in the region of £100,000, for himself and spent much of it on luxury items for his own benefit.

While he was acting in this way, the appellant, it was common ground, devised a form called a Bank 1 form, on which to record payments made by him to THB. At the original trial, the judge had ordered disclosure of Bank 1 forms by the prosecution but, save for one example of such a form, which was in the

b appellant's possession at the time of the first trial, no such disclosure had been made. Between the first trial and the retrial, however, those documents, which had apparently been in the possession not of the prosecuting authorities but of THB, were disclosed to the defence and were available to them at the time of the retrial.

A submission was made to the trial judge, Judge Crush, by Mr Willers then, as now, appearing for the defendant, that the second trial should be stayed as an

c abuse of the process of the court. The ground of that submission was that it would not be fair to try the appellant a second time, because the Bank 1 forms had not been available during the first trial and, if they had been, the first jury might have acquitted. The learned judge rejected that submission. That rejection forms the ground of appeal in relation to which the single judge gave leave and which Mr

d Willers has placed in the forefront of his argument in this court.

Mr Willers accepts that, although the judge at the first trial ordered disclosure and no disclosure took place, that was because the documents had simply not at that stage been found, although they were in the possession of THB.

Mr Willers did not, during the course of the first trial, make any further application, non-disclosure not having been made, either for the jury to be

e discharged, or otherwise.

Mr Willers does not suggest that, at the first trial or subsequently, there was any bad faith on the part of the prosecution in relation to the non-disclosure. He submits that, during the cross-examination of Det Sgt James at the second trial, it emerged that he had left with THB the responsibility for looking through the vast

f number of documents and passing to the police those which they thought relevant. Although Mr Willers does not suggest that gave rise to bad faith by the officer, he submits that it would have been better had the officer looked through the documents himself.

By the time of the second trial, however, Mr Willers accepts that the defence had all the documentation that they required, including all the Bank 1 forms. But,

g he submits, if there was a real possibility of acquittal at the first trial had those forms then been available, it was unfair for the second trial to take place, and the judge should have acceded to the defence application to stay the second trial for abuse of process.

Mr Willers accepted that his submission came to this that, despite the fact that

h all the relevant material was before the second jury who convicted, this court, in ruling upon the safety of that conviction, should speculate that the first jury, faced with all the relevant material, might have acquitted; and therefore it was unfair to proceed with the second trial. Mr Willers referred to the decision of this court in *R v Chalkley, R v Jeffries* [1998] 2 All E.R. 155, [1998] QB 848. In the course of giving the judgment of the court in that case, Auld LJ commented, adversely, on an

j earlier decision of this court, differently constituted, in *R v Bloomfield* [1997] 1 Cr App R 135, which had attracted some criticism from the editors of the third supplement to *Archbold's Criminal Pleading, Evidence and Practice* (1997 edn) para 7–45. We make that comment because the argument originally advanced in skeleton form on behalf of the appellant relied, in part, on this court's decision in *R v Bloomfield*.

On behalf of the Crown, Mr Davies submits that the safety of the appellant's *a* conviction depends on the evidence at the second trial, which was followed by an admirably succinct summing up by the learned judge, following a trial which, for reasons which are not manifest, had lasted a considerable number of weeks.

Mr Davies draws attention, in relation to the safety of that conviction, to a number of letters written by the appellant after these apparent defalcations came to light, the first of them, it was common ground, on 21 March 1994 to a man *b* called Andrew Orchard. That letter was written on the day that the defendant left this country, for a period of some seven months in the Canary Islands. The appellant also wrote letters to his sister, Jackie, and to his partner, David. Each of those letter, in various ways, comprises a series of admissions of criminal mis-behaviour of present materiality, coupled with expressions of regret. In the course of the thal, the appellant sought to explain those letters away on the basis of a state of *c* confused mind when he had written them.

In our judgment, it is wholly impossible to accept Mr Willers' submission either that the judge was wrong to rule as he did in refusing a stay, or that that refusal gives rise to any lack of safety in this appellant's conviction. It frequently happens that new evidence comes to light between the time of a first trial when a jury *d* disagrees and a second trial. Such evidence may be favourable to the prosecution or to the defence. But the verdict of the second jury does not become unsafe because it was unfair for there to be a second trial. Indeed, pursuing Mr Willers' argument to its logical conclusion, wherever fresh evidence appears between a first and second trial, it would be unfair, at least if the evidence assisted the defence, to have a second trial at all. That is a submission which we roundly reject. *e* The learned judge was, in our view, correct to refuse the stay on the basis of the application made to him. That refusal, in the light of the overwhelming evidence before the second jury, cannot, in any event, be regarded as rendering the verdict of the second jury unsafe.

The second matter which Mr Willers sought to canvass related to a criticism of the *f* learned judge's direction in relation to dishonesty and the character of the defence case. It is said that the judge misdirected the jury and failed to put the defence case adequately in relation to the way in which money was spent on luxuries.

It is fair to say that Mr Willers sought the leave of this court to pursue the interrelated grounds in relation to that aspect of the case, the learned single judge having refused leave to argue those grounds. For the avoidance of doubt, where, *g* in granting leave to appeal on some grounds, the single judge has specifically refused leave to appeal on other grounds, the leave of this court is required before counsel may argue those other grounds. As we have said, Mr Willers sought the leave of this court. We have read the passage in the summing up in the transcript of which he complains. It is to be noted that, in answer to a question from the *h* jury, the judge gave a dear direction as to dishonesty, relevant to this case, in identical terms to that which he had given at the outset of his summing up.

Nothing in the passage of the summing up about which complaint is made, in our view, renders it arguable that there was any misdirection. Accordingly, as to that aspect of the case, we refused leave to pursue an appeal on that basis. *i*

For the reasons given, this appeal is dismissed.

Appeal dismissed.

Carlone Stomberg   Barrister.

The case is the criminal law case of *R. v Jackson*. Lawyers pronounce this "Regina (or 'The Queen' or 'King', or 'The Crown') against Jackson". Most criminal cases are written like this. In civil cases, the names of the parties are usually given, as in *Donoghue v Stevenson*, the case being pronounced "Donoghue and Stevenson".

Underneath the name of the case at "**a**" you will see three pieces of information. First, you are told the court in which the case was heard. In this case, it was the Court of Appeal, Criminal Division. It is important to know which court heard a case because of the doctrine of precedent (see pp.107–110 for an explanation of the doctrine of precedent).

The report then gives the names of the judges who took part in the case. This information is used to help evaluate the decision. Some judges are known to be very experienced in particular areas of law. Their decisions may be given extra weight. Finally, you are told when the case was heard and when the court gave its decision. In the House of Lords this process is called "delivering opinions", but in other courts it is known as "giving judgment".

The material in italics, at "**b**" on the first page of the report, is written by the editor of the report. It indicates the subject matter of the case and the issue which it concerned. The subject index at the front of each volume of law reports includes a similar entry under the first words.

The next section, at "**c**", is called the *headnote*. It is not part of the case proper, and is prepared by the law reporter, not by the judges. The headnote should summarise the case accurately giving references to important parts of the court's opinion or judgment and any cases cited. Because it is written when the case is reported, the headnote may stress or omit elements of the case which are later thought to be important. Therefore, care should be taken when using the headnote.

The notes, just below "**d**", direct the reader to appropriate volumes of *Halsbury's Laws of England* and/or *Halsbury's Statutes of England*. *Halsbury's Laws* provides a concise statement of the relevant law, subject by subject, including references to the main cases and statutes. *Halsbury's Statutes* gives the complete text of all statutes together with annotations that explain them. Although law students and others may need to research the law using *Halsbury* it is not necessary to turn to reference works when reading every case. In most instances, the background law will be sufficiently explained by the judge. In our case of *R. v Jackson* the reference is confined to *Halsbury's Laws*.

At "**e**" there is a list of all the cases referred to by the judges. In relation to each case, a list of different places where the case may be found is given. Where counsel have cited additional cases to which the judges did not refer, this will be given in a separate list under the heading "cases also cited".

At "**e**" to "**f**" you will find a full history of the proceedings of the case. This indicates all the courts that have previously considered the case before the present one. The final sentence of this section indicates where a full account of the facts of the case may be found.

Below "**f**" you will find the names of the counsel (usually barristers but sometimes solicitor-advocates) who appeared in the case. In the case of *R. v Jackson* the barristers on both sides were what are known as "junior counsel". Senior counsel are called "QCs" (Queen's Counsel), or "KCs" (King's Counsel) when the monarch is a King.

The appellant was Jackson, while the Crown (in other words the state) was the respondent. The names of the solicitors who acted for the two parties and instructed the counsel are to be found below "**f**" in the law report. Academics may use this information to obtain further information about the case. Solicitors may use it in order to find out which are the best counsel to instruct for particular kinds of cases.

Not all series of law reports have marginal letters as this one does. When they do, these letters can be used to give a precise reference to any part of the case. Thus, the beginning of Lord Justice Rose's judgment is [1999] 1 All E.R. 572g.

Whilst the matters above provide an introduction to the case, the substance is to be found in the judgments. Every law case raises a question or series of questions to be answered by the judge(s). In civil cases, some of these will be questions of fact (in criminal cases these will be answered by the jury). For example, it may be necessary to know at what speed a car was travelling when an accident occurred. In practice, the answers to these factual questions are very important. Once they have been settled, the legal issues in the case may be simple. However, when it comes to the study of law, it is only the legal questions that matter.

For the judge(s) in a case, therefore, there are two clearly distinguishable processes which have to be gone through when hearing the matter and reaching a judgment. First, there is the process of making "findings of fact". Then, in the light of those findings of fact, there is the process of making "findings on the law". The key questions that are posed to the judge(s) in this context are referred to as "the issues in the case".

Lawyers and students of law are concerned primarily not with the outcome of a case but with the reasoning that the judge gave for the conclusion. The reasoning is important because within it will be found the *ratio decidendi* (often referred to simply as "the ratio"). The ratio is that part of the legal reasoning which is essential for the decision in the case. It is the ratio which is binding under the doctrine of precedent and which is thus part of the law. The ratio and the reasons for the decision are not necessarily the same thing. Not all of the reasons given for the decision will be essential. In courts where there is more than one judge, each may give a separate judgment (as can be seen from the examples in the exercises section of this book). If they do, each judgment will have its own reasons, and thus its own ratio. The judges must agree a conclusion to the case (although they may do so only by majority). However, they do not have to have the same reasons for their decision. If they have different reasons the judgments have different ratios and, thus, the case itself may have no ratio. Lawyers will rarely agree that a case has no ratio at all.

Finding the ratio in a case is crucial. It is also the most difficult part of reading cases, particularly when the case involves several judgments. The ratio is the essence of the case and, thus, may not be found simply by quoting from a judgment. Discovering the ratio involves skills of interpretation—understanding and explaining what judges meant, how they reached their conclusions—in order to see the common ground. Although the ratio is the law, it cannot be divorced entirely from the facts. Facts that are essential for a decision to provide the conditions for the operation of the rules and are, thus, part of the rule itself. Deciding which are essential, as opposed to subsidiary, facts takes skill and practice. Lawyers frequently disagree on exactly what the ratio to a decision is. Some may view it broadly, seeing the decision as having few conditions but laying down a general rule. Others may take a narrower approach, suggesting that only in very limited circumstances would a decision bind a future court. Subsequent cases often help to clarify what the ratio of a previous case is accepted as being. There is a more detailed explanation of the way in which one decides what the ratio of a case is in Chapter 6 below.

The editors of a law report write what they consider the ratio to be in the headnote. They may be wrong. Even if their interpretation is plausible when they write it, a later case may take a different view. For these reasons, statements of law in the headnote cannot be relied on.

If we look at *R. v Jackson* we can see that some of the things that we are told in the judgment are irrelevant for the purposes of constructing the ratio. The case before the Court of Appeal concerns a question relating to "leave to appeal". Thus, for example, the fact that the accused collected money on a weekly basis, rather than monthly, is of no account. Similarly, the fact that he failed to declare to the insurance brokers the full amount that he had collected is not significant for the purposes of the Court of Appeal on the question concerning "leave to appeal". However, we will be aware that, for the original trial judge in the Crown Court, when the charges brought against the accused were of "false accounting", this would have been a very significant matter.

You will see that in the case of *R. v Jackson* Lord Justice Rose (Rose LJ) delivers a judgment that is the "judgment of the court". This therefore reflects the shared views of himself, Lord Justice Butterfield and Lord Justice Richards. Judgments in courts with multiple judges like the Court of Appeal and the Supreme Court are not always like this. Each judge may give their own judgment. Having set out the history of the case (at p.572 g–h), Lord Justice Rose then gives a brief outline of the relevant facts for the purposes of the appeal (at p.572h–573d). This is followed by a summary of the submissions made by the counsel for each party (at p.573d–574c). You will see that counsel are said to have "submitted" certain things and to have "accepted" other matters during the course of their arguments before the Court of Appeal. Having dealt with these matters by way of preliminary presentation, Lord Justice Rose then moves on to the conclusions of the Court of Appeal. It is here that we look for the reasons and the ratio in the case.

The first matter considered (set out at p.574c–e) is the court's view on a proposition put by counsel for the appellant. You will gather that the Court of Appeal has little sympathy for the argument put forward, and in quite strong terms (at p.574e) "roundly rejects" the proposition that "wherever fresh evidence appears between a first and second trial, it would be unfair, at least if the evidence assisted the defence, to have a second trial". This leads the Court of Appeal to the conclusion that (i) the trial judge acted correctly in refusing to "stay" the trial of the accused, and (ii) anyway, given the evidence before the second jury in this case, that the verdict of that second jury could not be regarded as in any way "unsafe" (see p.574e–f). These conclusions are specific to this case, although the first one follows from the view expressed by the court on counsel's (roundly rejected) proposition. The narrow ratio of the case may thus be discovered by looking at that view, which was essential for reaching the eventual decision delivered by the Court of Appeal.

However, it is the "second matter" dealt with by the Court of Appeal that has drawn the attention of the law report editor to this case. At p.574f–g you will see that the court is faced with a question of what permission (or "leave") is required in order for an appeal to be made against particular aspects of a case. The eventual decision of the Court of Appeal (not to allow an appeal to be pursued on the basis of an alleged misdirection in the trial judge's summing up) is set out at p.574j, and the reasons for arriving at this decision are explained at p.574h. In order to reach that decision, the court has had to decide in what circumstances an appeal such as this may or may not be pursued. In this case the Court of Appeal goes further than to pronounce merely in relation to the specific case before it, relating to Jackson, the accused. Here, the court makes a general statement "for the avoidance of doubt", which is intended to clarify the situation for all future cases where this issue arises (set out at p.574g–h). That ratio, indeed, is also the part of the judgment that has been extracted by the editor of the law reports series to form the headnote that we have already looked at (at p.572c).

R. v Jackson contains only a single judgment. That judgment is a short one. If one had a longer judgment (and most judgments are longer) or multiple judgments in the same case, the task of constructing a ratio would be much more difficult. When one has to consider one judgment and its obscurities in the light of other judgments the process of analysing the law becomes even more uncertain. In order to appreciate some of the problems of constructing a ratio in a less straightforward case, therefore, you should apply the techniques discussed here to the law reports contained in the exercises section of this book.

A court must follow the ratio of any relevant case that is binding on it under the doctrine of precedent. Thus, the question arises, when is a case relevant? A case in the same area must be followed unless it can be "distinguished" on the basis of its facts. If the facts of the case cannot be distinguished—if, as it is commonly put, the case is "on all fours"—then it must be followed. The process of distinguishing cases is really just another way of deciding what the ratio of the case is. If the material facts necessary for the operation of the legal rule in the first case are not found in the second, or are different, there is no precedent. Just as lawyers differ about what the ratio to a case is, so they differ about whether a case is binding in a particular situation or not.

That which is not part of the ratio of the case is said to be the *obiter dictum*. This is usually referred to as "the *obiter*". Obiter is said to have "persuasive authority". That which was said obiter in a court such as the House of Lords may be very persuasive indeed for a relatively inferior court such as a County Court. Moreover, remarks made obiter may indicate which way the law is develop-ing, or which kinds of arguments judges find particularly persuasive. Equally, judges are not always very careful about differentiating between ratio and obiter. There is a further explanation of the place of obiter observations in legal reasoning in Chapter 6 below.

The remainder of this section provides some guidance on how to study cases. The first ques-tion a student should ask about a case is "Why has this case been set?" The purpose of studying cases is to obtain an understanding of the relevance of the case to the area of law being studied. Some cases will be more important than others. A leading Supreme Court decision will require more time and closer examination than a decision of the High Court that is merely illustrative of a point mentioned in a lecture or included in a problem. Where a case has developed or defined an area of law it is usually helpful to start by reading what the textbook writers say about it. Where more than one case has to be read on the same point of law, they should, if possible, be read in chronological order and each one digested before moving on to the next.

A second question to ask when reading cases is, "How much time is available?" Try to spend more time on important decisions and important judgments, even if you have to rely on a head-note or a textbook when it comes to the others. Do not spend the greater proportion of your time reading cases which have been overruled or which have novel or interesting facts but no new point of law. The headnote is helpful when allocating time. Treat judgments in the same way as you treat cases. Do not waste your time reading judgments that merely repeat something you have already read. Spend more time on the leading judgments than on the others. Again, the headnote will be helpful for this. Some judgments are more clearly written than others. Some judgments are shorter than others. Neither clarity nor brevity necessarily means that the judgment is more important. Choose what you read because it is the best for your purposes, not because it is the easiest!

Notes on any case should start with the case name and any references. They should then include:

(1) a brief statement of the facts of the case;
(2) the history of the case;
(3) the point of law under consideration;
(4) the decision with the reasons for it, together with any names of cases relied upon.

One page should be enough for this basic information.

When reading judgments in order to make notes, look for agreement and disagreement on each of the points relevant to your study. It is often useful to make separate notes on each of the points raised by the case and then see what different judges said about them. In particular, too, do not forget to make it clear in your notes whether a judge was dissenting or not.

HOW TO READ A STATUTE

This section will explain how you should read statutes. The way in which statutes are created is explained on pp.4–5. Looking for a particular legal rule in a statute can be confusing. Some statutes are over 100 pages long, although most are shorter. The language they use often appears complicated and obscure. If you understand the structure of a statute and follow a few simple rules in reading them, statutes will become much clearer. ▶ 5.3

A copy of a statute, the House of Lords Act 1999, is reproduced below. All subsequent references here are to this statute.

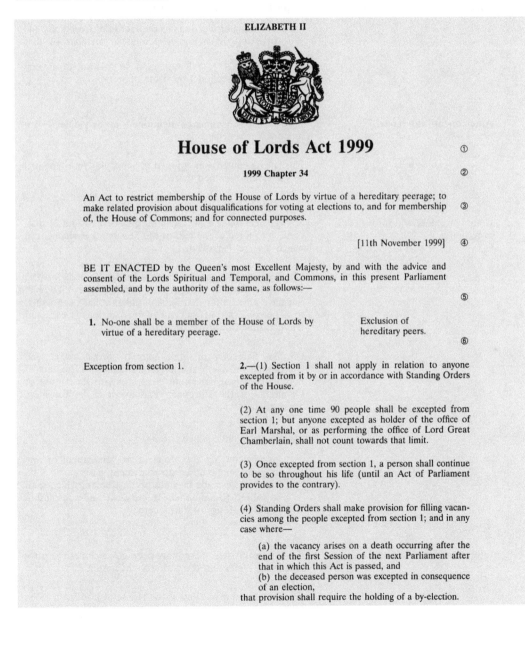

ELIZABETH II

House of Lords Act 1999 ①

1999 Chapter 34 ②

An Act to restrict membership of the House of Lords by virtue of a hereditary peerage; to make related provision about disqualifications for voting at elections to, and for membership of, the House of Commons; and for connected purposes. ③

[11th November 1999] ④

BE IT ENACTED by the Queen's most Excellent Majesty, by and with the advice and consent of the Lords Spiritual and Temporal, and Commons, in this present Parliament assembled, and by the authority of the same, as follows:—

⑤

1. No-one shall be a member of the House of Lords by virtue of a hereditary peerage.   Exclusion of hereditary peers.

⑥

Exception from section 1.   **2.**—(1) Section 1 shall not apply in relation to anyone excepted from it by or in accordance with Standing Orders of the House.

(2) At any one time 90 people shall be excepted from section 1; but anyone excepted as holder of the office of Earl Marshal, or as performing the office of Lord Great Chamberlain, shall not count towards that limit.

(3) Once excepted from section 1, a person shall continue to be so throughout his life (until an Act of Parliament provides to the contrary).

(4) Standing Orders shall make provision for filling vacancies among the people excepted from section 1; and in any case where—

(a) the vacancy arises on a death occurring after the end of the first Session of the next Parliament after that in which this Act is passed, and
(b) the deceased person was excepted in consequence of an election,
that provision shall require the holding of a by-election.

(5) A person may be excepted from section 1 by or in accordance with Standing Orders made in anticipation of the enactment or commencement of this section.

(6) Any question whether a person is excepted from section 1 shall be decided by the Clerk of the Parliaments, whose certificate shall be conclusive.

Removal of disqualifications in relation to the House of Commons.

3.—(1) The holder of a hereditary peerage shall not be disqualified by virtue of that peerage for—

(a) voting at elections to the House of Commons, or
(b) being, or being elected as, a member of that House.

(2) Subsection (1) shall not apply in relation to anyone excepted from section 1 by virtue of section 2.

Amendments and repeals.

4.—(1) The enactments mentioned in Schedule 1 are amended as specified there.

(2) The enactments mentioned in Schedule 2 are repealed to the extent specified there.

Commencement and transitional provision.

5.—(1) Sections 1 to 4 (including Schedules 1 and 2) shall come into force at the end of the Session of Parliament in which this Act is passed.

(2) Accordingly, any writ of summons issued for the present Parliament in right of a hereditary peerage shall not have effect after that Session unless it has been issued to a person who, at the end of the Session, is excepted from section 1 by virtue of section 2.

(3) The Secretary of State may by order make such transitional provision about the entitlement of holders of hereditary peerages to vote at elections to the House of Commons or the European Parliament as he considers appropriate.

(4) An order under this section—

(a) may modify the effect of any enactment or any provision made under an enactment, and
(b) shall be made by statutory instrument which shall be subject to annulment in pursuance of a resolution of either House of Parliament.

Interpretation and short title.

6.—(1) In this Act "hereditary peerage" includes the principality of Wales and the earldom of Chester.

(2) This Act may be cited as the House of Lords Act 1999.

SCHEDULES

SCHEDULE 1

AMENDMENTS

Peerage Act 1963 (c.48)

1. In section 1(2) of the Peerage Act 1963 (disclaimer of certain hereditary peerages) for the words from "has" to the end there shall be substituted the words "is excepted from section 1 of the House of Lords Act 1999 by virtue of section 2 of that Act".

Recess Elections Act 1975 (c.66)

2. In section 1 of the Recess Elections Act 1975 (issue of warrants for making out writs to replace members of the House of Commons whose seats have become vacant), in—

    (a) subsection (1)(a), and

    (b) paragraph (a) of the definition of "certificate of vacancy" in subsection (2),

    for the words "become a peer" there shall be substituted the words "become disqualified as a peer for membership of the House of Commons".

SCHEDULE 2

REPEALS

Chapter	Short title	Extent of repeal
1963 c.48.	The Peerage Act 1963.	In section 1(3), paragraph (b) and the word "and" immediately preceding it. Section 2. In section 3, in subsection (1)(b), the words from "(including" to "that House)" and, in subsection (2), the words from "and" to the end of the subsection. Section 5.

Statutes are available online at a number of different websites (see, for example, *http://www. statutelaw.gov.uk/, http://www.legislation.gov.uk/ukpga* and *http://www.bailii.org/*). These are open-access online databases. Commercial services such as WestLaw also have statutes online. In the present day online services is one of the ways that you are most likely to get access to a statute. The other way, as a student, that you may read a statute is in a hardcopy collection of statutes in a particular area of law that has been commercially published. In the case of both hard-copy collections and online services statutes are sometimes published in an annotated form. This means that the statute has an accompanying explanatory text that tells you what the statute means. If you use an annotated statute remember that only the words of the statute are definitive. The explanatory text, although it may be helpful in understanding the statute, is only ever the opinion of the author.

THE DIFFERENT PARTS

5.4 ▶ ① This is the *short title* of the Act, together with its year of publication. When you are writing about a statute, it is normal to use the short title and year of publication to describe the statute. Sometimes, when a statute is referred to constantly, the short title is abbreviated. Thus, the Matrimonial Causes Act 1973 is often referred to as "the MCA 1973". If you work in a particular area of law, you will quickly learn the standard abbreviations for that area.

② This is the official *citation* for the statute. Each Act passed in any one year is given its own number. This is known as its *chapter number*. Thus you can describe a statute by its chapter number and year. The citation "1999 Chapter 34" could only mean the House of Lords Act 1999. "Chapter" in the official citation may be abbreviated to "c.", as in the top right hand corner of your copy of the statute. This form of official citation began in 1963. Before that, statutes were identified by the "regnal year" in which they occurred, followed by their chapter number. A regnal year is a year of a monarch's reign. Thus, "30 Geo 3 Chapter 3" refers to the Treason Act 1790, which was passed in the 30th year of King George III's reign. It is much easier to remember and use the short title of an Act rather than its official citation.

③ This is the *long title* of the Act. The long title gives some indication of the purpose behind the Act. It may be of some use in deciding what the Act is all about. However, the long title may be misleading. For example, the long title of the Parliament Act 1911 indicates that the Act is part of a process of abolishing the House of Lords—although, over 100 years later, that institution is still in existence, even though the House of Lords Act 1999 has introduced restrictions upon membership of the institution by virtue of a hereditary peerage. Long titles are sometimes vague and may conflict with the main body of the Act. In the event of such a conflict, the legal rule is that expressed in the main body of the Act.

④ This indicates when the *royal assent* was given and the House of Lords Bill 1999 became an Act. Statutes become law on the date when they receive the royal assent *unless the Act says otherwise*. The statute itself may say that it becomes law on a fixed date after the royal assent, or it may give a Government Minister the power to decide when it becomes law. When a Minister brings a statute into effect after the date on which it has been passed a "commencement order" must be made. This is a form of delegated legislation. Statutes do not have a retrospective effect unless the Act expressly says so.

⑤ This is known as the *enacting formula*. It is the standard form of words used to indicate that a Bill has been properly passed by all the different parts of the legislature.

⑥ By each section you will find a short explanation of the content of that section. These *marginal notes* may help you to understand the content of the section if it is otherwise unclear.

The main body of the statute that follows is broken up into numbered *sections*. Each section contains a different rule of law. When you refer to a rule of law contained in a statute, you should say where that rule of law is to be found. This enables others to check your source and to see whether or not they agree with your interpretation of the law. Instead of writing "section", it is usual to abbreviate this to "s.". Thus, "section 1" becomes "s.1". Sections are often further subdivided. These sub-division are known as *subsections*. When you wish to refer to a subsection, you should add it in brackets after the main section.

In larger statutes, sections may be grouped together into different *Parts*. Each Part will deal with a separate area of law. Looking for the correct Part will help you to find the particular legal rule that you want.

Some statutes have one or more *Schedules* at the end. The content of these varies. Some contain detailed provisions that are not found in the main body of the act. Others are merely convenient reminders and summaries of legal rules, and changes to legal rules, found elsewhere in the Act.

In the House of Lords Act 1999, for example, there are two Schedules. The first Schedule says which sections of previous statutes have been changed (amended) by the 1999 Act. This Schedule sets out the detailed effect of the amendments, which are given their legal effect by virtue of s.4(1) of the Act. The second Schedule sets out which sections of a previous statute have been repealed by the 1999 Act. Those repeals are given their legal effect by virtue of s.4(2) of the Act.

> **Example**
>
> Q. *How many people are excepted from s.1 of the House of Lords Act 1999? A. 90 people at any one time. See s.2(2) House of Lords Act 1999.*

References to Schedules are often abbreviated as "Sched.". Where a Schedule is divided up, the divisions are known as *paragraphs*, and can be abbreviated as "para.".

USING A STATUTE

Your use of statutory material will vary. Sometimes you will be referred to a particular section or sections of a statute in a case, article, or book that you are reading. In other instances, a new statute will be passed which you need to assess as a whole in order to see how it affects those areas of law in which you are interested. In either case, when first reading statutory material, you may be able to gain some help in deciding what it means from commentaries.

▶ 5.5

Commentaries are explanations of the law written by legal academics or practitioners. Annotated statutes, which were discussed earlier, are one useful source of such commentaries. You may also find such commentaries in books and articles on the area of law in which the statute falls. Always remember that a commentary represents only one author's opinion of what the statute says. In the case of a very new statute there will probably be no commentary. Therefore, you will need to be able to read a statute yourself, so that you can assess the value of other people's opinions and form your own view when there is no other help available.

When reading a statute, do not begin at the beginning and then work your way through to the end, section by section. Statutes do not necessarily use words to mean the same things that they do in ordinary conversation. Before you can decide what a statute is about you need to know if there are any special meanings attached to words in it. These special meanings can be found in the Act, often in sections called *definition* or *interpretation sections*. These are frequently found towards the end of the Act. For example, in the House of Lords Act 1999, there is a guide in s.6(1) to the interpretation of the expression "hereditary peerage" when used in the context of the Act. An Act may have more than one definition section. Sometimes, Parliament, when laying down a particular meaning for a word, will say that the specified meaning will apply in all statutes in which that word appears. Unless a statute specifically says this, however, you should assume that a definition in a statute applies only the use of the word in that statute.

You are now in a position to decide what new legal rules the statute creates. Some people begin this task by reading the long title of the Act to give themselves some idea of the general aim of the statute. Although this can be helpful, as we saw above in the section on the different parts of the Act, it can also be misleading.

Statutes should be read carefully and slowly. The general rule is that a statute means precisely what it says. Each word is important. Because of this, some words that we use loosely in ordinary conversation take on special significance when found in a statute. For example, it is important to distinguish between words like "may" and "shall", one saying that you *can* do something and the other saying that you *must* do something. Conjunctives, such as "and", joining things together, must be distinguished from disjunctives, such as "or", dividing things apart.

So far, the emphasis has been upon closely reading the particular statute. You should also remember that the statute should be read in the context of the general Acts, rules and principles of statutory interpretation discussed in Chapter 7.

One further thing to remember when reading a statute is that the fact that it has been printed does not mean that it is part of the law of the land. It may have been repealed. It may not yet be in force. Re-read pp.34–35 if you cannot remember how to find out if a statute has been repealed. Go back and read about the royal assent on p.50 if you cannot remember how to find out if a statute is in force.

STATUTORY INSTRUMENTS

5.6 ▶ What statutory instruments are, the way in which they are created, and the purposes that they have, are discussed on p.4.

Statutory instruments should be read in the same way as statutes. However, whilst statutes make relatively little reference to other sources, statutory instruments, because of their purpose, make very frequent reference either to other statutory instruments or to their parent statute. The legislative power has been given only for a limited purpose, the statutory instrument is a small part of a larger whole. For this reason, you will find it much more difficult to understand a statutory instrument if you do not have access to the surrounding legislation. Before reading a statutory instrument, it is vital that you understand the legislative framework into which it fits.

Exercise 1

STATUTES I

Start by re-reading the appropriate parts of Chapters 5 and 7 and then look at the Succession to   ▶ **5.7**
the Crown Act 2013 and answer the questions below. When answering the questions, make sure
you include the correct statutory references. Answers to Section A for each exercise can be found
in Appendix III.

ELIZABETH II   c. 20

Succession to the Crown Act 2013

2013 CHAPTER 20

An Act to make succession to the Crown not depend on gender; to make provision about Royal Marriages; and for connected purposes.

[25th April 2013]

BE IT ENACTED by the Queen's most Excellent Majesty, by and with the advice and consent of the Lords Spiritual and Temporal, and Commons, in this present Parliament assembled, and by the authority of the same, as follows: —

1 Succession to the Crown not to depend on gender

In determining the succession to the Crown, the gender of a person born after 28 October 2011 does not give that person, or that person's descendants, precedence over any other person (whenever born).

2 Removal of disqualification arising from marriage to a Roman Catholic

(1) A person is not disqualified from succeeding to the Crown or from possessing it as a result of marrying a person of the Roman Catholic faith.

(2) Subsection (1) applies in relation to marriages occurring before the time of the coming into force of this section where the person concerned is alive at that time (as well as in relation to marriages occurring after that time).

3 Consent of Sovereign required to certain Royal Marriages

(1) A person who (when the person marries) is one of the 6 persons next in the line of succession to the Crown must obtain the consent of Her Majesty before marrying.

(2) Where any such consent has been obtained, it must be—
   (a) signified under the Great Seal of the United Kingdom,
   (b) declared in Council, and
   (c) recorded in the books of the Privy Council.

(3) The effect of a person's failure to comply with subsection (1) is that the person and the person's descendants from the marriage are disqualified from succeeding to the Crown.

(4) The Royal Marriages Act 1772 (which provides that, subject to certain exceptions, a descendant of King George II may marry only with the consent of the Sovereign) is repealed.

(5) A void marriage under that Act is to be treated as never having been void if—
    (a) neither party to the marriage was one of the 6 persons next in the line of succession to the Crown at the time of the marriage,
    (b) no consent was sought under section 1 of that Act, or notice given under section 2 of that Act, in respect of the marriage,
    (c) in all the circumstances it was reasonable for the person concerned not to have been aware at the time of the marriage that the Act applied to it, and
    (d) no person acted, before the coming into force of this section, on the basis that the marriage was void.

(6) Subsection (5) applies for all purposes except those relating to the succession to the Crown.

4 Consequential amendments etc

(1) The Schedule contains consequential amendments.

(2) References (however expressed) in any enactment to the provisions of the Bill of Rights or the Act of Settlement relating to the succession to, or possession of, the Crown are to be read as including references to the provisions of this Act.

(3) The following enactments (which relate to the succession to, and possession of, the Crown) are subject to the provision made by this Act—
    Article II of the Union with Scotland Act 1706;
    Article II of the Union with England Act 1707;
    Article Second of the Union with Ireland Act 1800;
    Article Second of the Act of Union (Ireland) 1800.

5 Commencement and short title

(1) This section comes into force on the day on which this Act is passed.

(2) The other provisions of this Act come into force on such day and at such time as the Lord President of the Council may by order made by statutory instrument appoint.

(3) Different days and times may be appointed for different purposes.

(4) This Act may be cited as the Succession to the Crown Act 2013.

SCHEDULE

Section 4

CONSEQUENTIAL AMENDMENTS

Treason Act 1351

1   The Treason Act 1351 (declaration of offences to be adjudged treason) has effect as if—

(a)   the first reference to eldest son and heir were a reference to eldest child and heir;

(b)   the second reference to eldest son and heir were a reference to eldest son if the heir.

Bill of Rights

2   In section 1 of the Bill of Rights, omit—

(a)   "or by any King or Queene marrying a papist";

(b)   "or shall marry a papist";

(c)   "or marrying".

Act of Settlement

3   In the Act of Settlement—

(a)   in the preamble, omit "or marry a papist" and "or marrying";

(b)   in section 2, omit "or shall marry a papist".

Regency Act 1937

4   In section 3(2) of the Regency Act 1937 (persons disqualified from becoming or being Regent), after "Crown" insert ", or is a person disqualified from succeeding to the Crown by virtue of section 3(3) of the Succession to the Crown Act 2013".

Supplementary

5   The amendments made by paragraphs 2 and 3 apply in relation to marriages occurring before the time of the coming into force of section 2 where the person concerned is alive at that time (as well as in relation to marriages occurring after that time).

Section A

1. What is the oldest statute that is amended by the 2015 Act?
2. When did the Act come into force?
3. What is the definition of Roman Catholic?
4. Who needs the Queen's consent to marry?

5. Can a person succeed to the Crown if they are married to a Roman Catholic?
6. What effect does gender have on succession to the Crown?

Section B

7. What is the short title of this Act?
8. Find out whether any regulations have been made under this Act.
9. Have there been any reported cases on the Act?
10. What is the reason why some people have to ask for the monarch's permission to marry?
11. If someone who is required to get the monarch's consent to marry does not do so and gets married anyway what effect does that have?
12. Why do you think the Act was passed?

Exercise 2

STATUTES II

5.8 ▶ Read the Child Care Act 2016 and answer the questions. When answering the questions make sure you include the correct statutory references. Answers to Section A for each exercise can be found in Appendix III.

Childcare Act 2016

2016 CHAPTER 5

An Act to make provision about free childcare for young children of working parents and about the publication of information about childcare and related matters by local authorities in England.   [16th March 2016]

B E IT ENACTED by the Queen's most Excellent Majesty, by and with the advice and consent of the Lords Spiritual and Temporal, and Commons, in this present Parliament assembled, and by the authority of the same, as follows:—

Availability of free childcare

1   Duty to secure 30 hours free childcare available for working parents

   (1)   The Secretary of State must secure that childcare is available free of charge for qualifying children of working parents for, or for a period equivalent to, 30 hours in each of 38 weeks in any year.

   (2)   "Qualifying child of working parents" means a young child—

      (a)   who is under compulsory school age,

      (b)   who is in England,

      (c)   who is of a description specified in regulations made by the Secretary of State,

      (d)   in respect of whom any conditions relating to a parent of the child, or a partner of a parent of the child, which are specified in such regulations, are met, and

      (e)   in respect of whom a declaration has been made, in accordance with such regulations, to the effect that the requirements of paragraphs (a) to (d) are satisfied.

   (3)   The conditions mentioned in subsection (2)(d) may, in particular, relate to the paid work undertaken by a parent or partner.

   (4)   For the purposes of subsections (2) and (3), the Secretary of State may by regulations—

(a) make provision about when a person is, or is not, to be regarded as another person's partner;

(b) make provision as to what is, or is not, paid work;

(c) specify circumstances in which a person is, or is not, to be regarded as in such work;

(d) make provision about—

    (i) the form of a declaration and the manner in which it is to be made;

    (ii) the conditions to be met by the person making a declaration;

    (iii) the period for which a declaration has effect.

(5) For the purposes of assisting the Secretary of State in the discharge of the duty imposed by subsection (1), the Commissioners for Her Majesty's Revenue and Customs may carry out functions in connection with the making of determinations as to whether a child is a qualifying child of working parents.

(6) In determining, for the purposes of subsection (1), the amount of childcare that is available—

(a) account is to be taken of any childcare available under the duty imposed by section 7(1) of the Childcare Act 2006 (duty of English local authorities to secure early years provision free of charge in accordance with regulations), but

(b) no account is to be taken of childcare available otherwise than by virtue of that duty or the duty imposed by subsection (1).

(7) The Secretary of State must set out in regulations when a year begins for the purposes of determining in relation to a child whether the duty in subsection (1) has been discharged.

(8) The Secretary of State may by regulations make provision about the circumstances in which a child is, or is not, in England for the purposes of this section.

(9) In this section—

"childcare" has the meaning given by section 18 of the Childcare Act 2006;

"parent", in relation to a child, includes any individual who—

    (a) has parental responsibility for the child, or

    (b) has care of the child;

"parental responsibility" has the same meaning as in the Children Act 1989;

"young child": a child is a "young child" during the period—

    (a) beginning with the child's birth, and

    (b) ending immediately before the 1 September next following the date on which the child attains the age of 5.

2 Discharging the section 1(1) duty

(1) The Secretary of State may make regulations for the purpose of discharging the duty imposed by section 1(1) ("extended entitlement regulations").

(2) Extended entitlement regulations may (amongst other things)—

(a) require an English local authority to secure that childcare of such a description as may be specified is made available free of charge for children in their area who are qualifying children of working parents;

      (b) make provision about how much childcare is to be so made available for each child, and about the times at which, and periods over which, that childcare is to be made available;

      (c) make provision about the terms of any arrangements made between English local authorities and providers or arrangers of childcare for the purposes of meeting any requirement imposed under paragraph (a) or (b);

      (d) impose obligations or confer powers on the Commissioners for Her Majesty's Revenue and Customs;

      (e) make provision requiring information or documents to be provided by a person to the Secretary of State, the Commissioners for Her Majesty's Revenue and Customs or an English local authority;

      (f) make provision for the purpose of enabling any person to check whether a child is a qualifying child of working parents;

      (g) for that purpose, make provision about the disclosure of information held by a Minister of the Crown, the Commissioners for Her Majesty's Revenue and Customs or an English local authority;

      (h) create criminal offences in connection with the onward disclosure of information obtained under paragraph (g) where that information relates to a particular person and is not disclosed in a way authorised by or specified in the regulations;

      (i) make provision for reviews of, or appeals to the First-tier Tribunal against, determinations relating to a child's eligibility for childcare under section 1;

      (j) make provision for a person specified in the regulations to impose financial penalties on persons in connection with —

           (i) false or misleading information provided, or statements made or provided, in connection with a determination of a child's eligibility for childcare under section 1, or

           (ii) dishonest conduct in connection with the process of making such a determination;

      (k) require English local authorities, when discharging their duties under the regulations, to have regard to any guidance given from time to time by the Secretary of State.

(3) Extended entitlement regulations which impose a duty, or confer a power, on the Commissioners for Her Majesty's Revenue and Customs, or authorise disclosure of information held by the Commissioners, may only be made with the consent of the Treasury.

(4) In relation to a criminal offence created by virtue of subsection (2)(h), extended entitlement regulations may not provide for a penalty of imprisonment on conviction on indictment greater than imprisonment for a term not exceeding two years (whether or not accompanied by a fine).

(5) If provision is made by virtue of subsection (2)(j) —

      (a) the maximum amount of any penalty that may be specified in, or determined in accordance with, the regulations is £3,000;

      (b) the regulations must include provision enabling a person on whom a financial penalty is imposed —

           (i) to require a review of the imposition of the penalty or its amount by the person who imposed the penalty;

           (ii) to appeal against the imposition of the penalty or its amount to the First-tier Tribunal.

(6)   The Secretary of State may by regulations substitute a different amount for the amount for the time being specified in subsection (5)(a).

(7)   In section 15 of the Childcare Act 2006 (powers of Secretary of State to secure proper performance of English local authorities' powers and duties under Part 1 of that Act) references to Part 1 of that Act are to be read as including a reference to section 1 and this section.

(8)   In this section —

"childcare" has the meaning given by section 18 of the Childcare Act 2006;

"English local authority" means —

(a)   a county council in England;

(b)   a metropolitan district council;

(c)   a non-metropolitan district council for an area for which there is no county council;

(d)   a London borough council;

(e)   the Common Council of the City of London (in their capacity as a local authority);

(f)   the Council of the Isles of Scilly;

"parent" has the same meaning as in section 1;

"qualifying child of working parents" has the meaning given by section 1(2).

3   Sections 1 and 2: consequential amendments

(1)   In section 99 of the Childcare Act 2006 (provision of information about young children: England), in subsection (1), omit the "and" at the end of paragraph (aa) and after paragraph (b) insert ", and

(c)   any other person who provides early years provision for the purposes of section 1(1) of the Childcare Act 2016 (Secretary of State's duty to secure 30 hours free childcare available for working parents),".

(2)   In Chapter 4 of Part 2 of the School Standards and Framework Act 1998 (financing of maintained schools) —

(a)   in section 45A (determination of specified budgets of local authority), after subsection (4B) insert —

"(4C)   For the purposes of this Part, a duty imposed on a local authority in England under section 2 of the Childcare Act 2016 (duties in connection with Secretary of State's duty to secure 30 hours free childcare for working parents) is also to be treated as an education function of the authority.";

(b)   in section 47ZA (free of charge early years provision outside a maintained school: budgetary framework: England), in subsection (3), for paragraph (a) (but not the "and" after it) substitute —

"(a)   for the purpose of the discharge of —

(i)   the authority's duty under section 7 of the Childcare Act 2006, or

(ii)   a duty imposed on the authority under section 2 of the Childcare Act 2016,".

4   Supplementary provision about regulations under sections 1 and 2

(1)   In this section "regulations" means regulations under section 1 or 2.

(2)   Regulations may —

    (a)   confer a discretion on any person;

    (b)   make different provision for different purposes;

    (c)   make consequential, incidental, supplemental, transitional or saving provision;

    (d)   amend, repeal or revoke any provision made by or under an Act (whenever passed or made).

(3)   Regulations are to be made by statutory instrument.

(4)   A statutory instrument containing (whether alone or with other provision) regulations mentioned in subsection (5) may not be made unless a draft of the instrument has been laid before and approved by a resolution of each House of Parliament.

(5)   The regulations referred to in subsection (4) are —

    (a)   the first regulations made under section 1;

    (b)   the first regulations made under section 2(1);

    (c)   any regulations under section 2(6);

    (d)   any other regulations that amend or repeal provision made by an Act.

(6)   Any other statutory instrument containing regulations is subject to annulment in pursuance of a resolution of either House of Parliament.

Publication of information

5   Duty to publish information about childcare and related matters

In section 12 of the Childcare Act 2006 (duty to provide information, advice and assistance), after subsection (6) insert —

"(6A)   Regulations may require each English local authority to publish information which is of a prescribed description and relates to any of the matters mentioned in paragraphs (a) to (c) of subsection (2).

(6B)   Regulations under subsection (6A) may require information to be published —

    (a)   at prescribed intervals;

    (b)   in a prescribed manner.

(6C)   Subsection (3) applies in relation to information prescribed under subsection (6A) as it applies in relation to information prescribed under subsection (2)."

General

6   Extent

This Act extends to England and Wales only.

7   Commencement

(1)   The following provisions come into force on the day on which this Act is passed—
  (a)   section 1(5);
  (b)   section 6;
  (c)   this section;
  (d)   section 8.

(2)   The remaining provisions of this Act come into force on such day or days as may be appointed by regulations made by the Secretary of State.

(3)   Regulations under subsection (2) may appoint different days for different purposes or different areas.

(4)   The Secretary of State may by regulations make transitional or saving provision in connection with the coming into force of any provision of this Act.

(5)   Regulations under this section are to be made by statutory instrument.

8   Short title

This Act may be cited as the Childcare Act 2016.

Section A

1. What is the purpose of the Child Care Act 2016?
2. When did the Act come into force?
3. What is a "Qualifying child of working parents"?
4. Does the Act create any criminal offences?
5. Under the Act does the Secretary of State have to make regulations regarding "extended entitlement"?
6. A child has been determined to be ineligible for childcare. Is there anything that can be done about this?

Section B

7. What is the maximum financial penalty for providing false or misleading information in connection with a determination of a child's eligibility for childcare under section 1 of the Act?
8. What is "paid work"?
9. Has childcare been regulated prior to this statute being passed?
10. Can an application for a childcare be made under the Act with respect to a child who is seven years old?
11. Why do local authorities have duties with respect to childcare rather than the national government?
12. What area of law governs the relationship between local authorities and individuals?

Exercise 3

CASES I

Begin by re-reading the appropriate parts of Chapters 4 and 5. After you have read *R v Henderson* ▶ **5.9**
answer the questions below. When noting your answers to the questions, you should include
reference(s) to the appropriate points in the judgment from which you have drawn your information. Answers to Section A questions are found in Appendix III.

Neutral Citation Number: [2016] EWCA Crim 965
No: 2015/1075/B4
IN THE COURT OF APPEAL
CRIMINAL DIVISION

Royal Courts of Justice
Strand
London, WC2A 2LL

Friday 27 May 2016

B e f o r e:
LORD JUSTICE HAMBLEN

MR JUSTICE JAY
-
HIS HONOUR JUDGE WAIT
(Sitting as a Judge of the CACD)

R E G I N A

V

CHRISTOPHER HENDERSON

Computer-Aided Transcript of the Stenograph Notes of
WordWave International Limited trading as DTI
165 Fleet Street   London EC4A 2DY
Tel No: 020 7404 1400 Fax No: 020 7404 1424
(Official Shorthand Writers to the Court)

Mr C Beyts appeared on behalf of the **Appellant**

Mr T Probert-Wood appeared on behalf of the **Crown**

J U D G M E N T
(Approved)

LORD JUSTICE HAMBLEN:

Introduction

1. On 1st December 2014, in the Crown Court at Isleworth before Recorder Peddie QC, the appellant was convicted of having an article with a blade, contrary to section 139(1) of the Criminal Justice Act 1988. He was acquitted of offences of possessing a disguised firearm (count 1) and possessing a false identity document with intent (count 2).

2. On 9th December 2014, before His Honour Judge Johnson, the appellant was sentenced to six months' imprisonment which was ordered to run consecutively to a sentence of five years' imprisonment for offences on other counts on the original indictment. The appellant appeals against conviction by leave of the single judge.

The outline facts

3. At about 6 am on 29th April 2014, police officers entered Flat 5, 64A The Broadway, London W13, where they found the appellant, his wife, their baby and the appellant's wife's brother. The police searched the premises and found in a room a bunch of keys which included the keys to the appellant's Ford Mondeo car. They also seized a stun gun (count 1) and a false French passport (count 2) which was found in a cupboard in the hallway. The appellant's car was parked in a communal car park at the rear of the flats which was agreed to be a public place. When the boot was searched PC King found a lock knife in a bag which contained baby changing items. The appellant was arrested and made no comment when later interviewed by the police in the presence of his solicitor.

4. The prosecution case was that the appellant had with him on 29th April 2014 in a public place, The Broadway W13, a bladed article, the lock knife.

5. The appellant gave evidence at trial that he was not in occupation of the flat and did not know the stun gun or passport were in it. He said that he did own a knife but that he had not put it in his car. He said that the knife was used by his wife to open cardboard cartons of what the judge recorded as Actimel, but might not have been that product. He said that he did not know that the knife was in the bag or that the bag was in the car. In cross-examination he confirmed that he was the only person who used the car.

The ruling on submission of no case to answer

6. In respect of count 3 a submission of no case was made on behalf of the appellant on the grounds that he was a considerable distance away from the car and therefore he did not have the lock knife "with him in a public place". The submission was rejected by the judge who accepted the prosecution case that the appellant had been in close contact with the lock knife "by virtue of it being in the car as opposed to distant from the vehicle."

The grounds of appeal

7. The grounds of appeal are that the conviction was unsafe because:

> (1) the judge erred in finding that the appellant could in law be guilty of having with him in a public place a bladed article;

> (2) the judge accordingly wrongly rejected the submission of no case to answer at the close of the prosecution case and wrongly left the case to the jury at the conclusion of all the evidence;

> (3) alternatively the judge failed to give the jury adequate directions on the particular facts of the case.

8. The appellant contends that the judge erred in law in finding that at the time of his arrest in a flat on the second floor of the building, it was open to the jury to find that the appellant "had with him in a public place" a knife which was in his car in the car park. In particular it is submitted that:

> (1) "having with" is much narrower than possession and requires an immediacy and physical presence which were lacking in the instant case; and

> (2) even though the knife was in a public place, the appellant was not and thus he did not have the knife with him in a public place or, if he did, this emphasises the inconsistency of the appellant having with him an item both in a public place and private place at the same time.

9. The respondent contends that:

> (1) whether the appellant had the knife with him as a matter of fact and degree was to be determined in each case;

> (2) on the facts of the instant case the appellant had ready access to the car keys and was only a matter of yards from the car and therefore had sufficient ready access to the knife to be capable of having it with him;

(3) the knife was in a public place, namely The Broadway, as alleged in the indictment.

10. In support of the appellant's case reliance is placed on two Scottish cases. In <u>McVey v Friel</u> 1996 SCCR 768 the issue was whether the defendant McVey had with him in a public place a firearm contrary to section 19 of the Firearms Act 1968. The facts were that police officers saw a loaded air rifle in McVey's car when it was parked outside his home at 8.30 in the morning. The appellant agreed to allow the police to search the car and opened the car door for them. The Sheriff convicted the appellant on the ground that he had the gun with him while he was in the house and that in any event he had it with him when he opened the car for the police. In his judgment, the Sheriff said as follows:

> ". . . I think the approach taken by the procurator fiscal depute has merit. The analogy drawn by him of a person in a friend's house regarding himself as 'having with him' a cassette in his car parked outside is in my view a good one. It seemed to me that the phrase 'has with him' if given its ordinary meaning can extend to situations such as this, where the article in question is in a car belonging to and under the control of the accused and the accused is in a house nearby. An ordinary person would in my view regard the accused as having the article with him ... I would in any event have upheld the submission on the basis that even if, while he was in the house, the appellant did not have the weapon with him, he had it with him when he was at the car, having opened the car."

11. The appeal was allowed by the Appeal Court but no opinions or reasons were given. The appellant relies on the fact of the successful appeal and the inferred rejection of the Sheriff's reasoning.

12. In <u>Smith v Vannet</u> 1998 SCCR 410 a cosh and a knife was in the defendant Smith's car which was about six feet away from him when he was stopped and searched by the police. The Appeal Court held that Smith had the weapons with him as they were readily available for use by him. The court's conclusion was explained in the following terms:

> "If we apply a purposive approach to the sections with which we have to deal, it appears to us that they are designed to prevent people in a public place having offensive weapons and knives available to them which they may be liable to use ... in his pocket the appellant had the keys to the car and the car was only some six feet away in a narrow lane in the early hours of the morning. The cosh was under the passenger seat and the knife under the driver's mat. These weapons would have been readily available to the

appellant for use in the lane had he wished to make use of them. In our view on the basis of these facts the Sheriff was entitled to conclude that the appellant had the cosh and knife with him in the lane."

13. In that judgment reference was made to and reliance placed upon this court's decisions in R v Kelt [1977] 1 WLR 1365 and R v Pawlicki and Swindell [1992] 1 WLR 827. In R v Kelt, Scarman LJ stated as follows at page 1369:

". . . the legislature has drawn a distinction between the person who has a firearm with him and a person who is in possession of a firearm ... The legislature must have had in mind that in regard to those offences where it is an offence for a person to have with him a firearm there must be a very close physical link and degree of immediate control over the weapon by the man alleged to have the firearm with him."

He further stated at page 1370:

". . . possession is not enough ... the law requires the evidence to go a stage further and to establish if the accused had it with him. Of course the classic case of having a gun with you is if you are carrying it, but even if you are not carrying it you may yet have it with you if it is immediately available to you. And if all that can be shown is possession in the sense that it is in your house or in a shed or somewhere where you have ultimate control, that is not enough."

14. In R v Pawlicki and R v Swindell the appellant Pawlicki drove to an auctioneer's showroom, parked outside, locked the car leaving three sawn-off shotguns inside and went into the auction room and stood a few feet from the appellant Swindell. Police officers who had been alerted to the possibility of a robbery arrested both appellants. A search of Pawlicki's car revealed the sawn-off shotguns. Both appellants were convicted inter alia of having the firearms with intent to commit an indictable offence, namely robbery, contrary to section 18(1) of the Firearms Act 1968, which provides that: "It is an offence for a person to have with him a firearm ... with intent to commit an indictable offence."

15. As summarised in the headnote it was held that "to have with him a firearm" within the meaning of section 18(1) of the Firearms Act 1968, imported an element of propinquity which was not required for mere possession but in considering that element the emphasis

was on the accessibility of the guns to those embarking on committing an indictable offence rather than on the exact distance between them and the guns. In the circumstances the guns were readily accessible to the appellants at the time they were about to commit a robbery and therefore there were no grounds for interfering with the conviction for an offence under section 18(1) of the Act of 1968.

16. As stated by Steyn LJ at page 831H to 832B:

> " ... the words 'to have with him a firearm' must derive their colour from the purpose of the Firearms Act 1968. That purpose, in broad terms, is to combat the use of the firearms in and about the commission of crime and to protect public safety. The legislative technique, in so far as it is relevant, involves prohibitions on possession of firearms, and prohibitions on having a firearm. It was intended to be a relatively comprehensive statute. It is submitted that a distance of 50 yards between the men and the guns placed the men beyond the ambit of section 18(1). If that proposition is accepted, the 1968 Act is less effective than one would have expected. It seems to us that a court order ought to try to make sense of the statute and its purpose. If this purposive approach is adopted, it will still be necessary to consider the element of propinquity. But the emphasis must not be so much on exact distances between the criminals and their guns but rather on the accessibility of those guns, judged in a common sense way in the context of criminals embarking on a joint enterprise to commit an indictable offence."

17. The authorities indicate that in determining whether a person has a weapon "with him", relevant considerations include the following:

(1) Possession of a weapon is a wider concept than having it "with him".

(2) Having a weapon "with him" is a wider concept than carrying it.

(3) The propinquity between the person and the weapon.

(4) Whether the weapon is immediately available to the person.

(5) The accessibility of the weapon.

(6) The context of any criminal enterprise embarked upon.

(7) The purpose of the applicable statute.

Decision

18. In the present case it is to be noted that:

(1) The appellant was not near his car, as the defendant was in Smith v Vannet. He was in a second floor flat a considerable distance away.

(2) There was no evidence that the appellant had shortly left or was shortly to return to the car, as was the case in R v Pawlicki.

(3) There was no evidence that the knife in the car was linked in any way to his presence in the flat on that day or at all, unlike in R v Pawlicki.

(4) There was no evidence linking the knife to any ongoing or indeed any criminal enterprise, unlike in R v Pawlicki.

(5) The facts are comparable to the case of McVey v Friel in which the appeal was allowed.

19. In this case there was no close geographical, temporal or purposive link between the knife which was in a public place and the appellant who was in a private flat. Nor do we consider that it can be said that the knife was immediately available or readily accessible to the appellant.

20. In the light of the considerations set out above we conclude that the appellant did not in law have the knife "with him".

Conclusion

21. For the reasons outlined above the judge should have accepted the defence submission of no case to answer. The conviction is unsafe and it must accordingly be quashed.

Section A

1. This case is reported at [2016] EWCA Crim 965. What does this mean?
2. What offence was the defendant convicted of in the Crown Court?
3. What was the error of law that the judge was said to have made in the Crown Court?
4. Why did the Court of Appeal uphold the appeal?
5. According to the Court of Appeal is possession of something a wider or narrower concept than having something with you?

Section B

6. Find out whether or not R v Henderson has been reported in any series of law reports other than that above. Use both hardcopy and web-based sources to do this.

7. Jane has a knife in her car. She parks the car outside a shop, locks it and goes into the shop. Is she guilty of the offence that Henderson was charged with? What previous decision or decisions, if any, would you cite in support of your argument?
8. On the basis of the reasoning in *R v Henderson* in law what does possession mean?
9. Suresh bought a knife. He then leant it to his wife Rashmi. Does he have possession of it?
10. In the judgement in *R v Henderson* reference is made to Lord Steyn's argument that the courts should, in issues like the one raised in the case, take a purposive approach to interpreting a statute. What is a purposive approach to statutory interpretation? What reasons are there for the court taking such an approach? Do you think there could be any problems if the courts do this?
11. If we accept that the use of knives in the course of committing crimes is a serious problem why do we not simply make the possessing of knives in a public place a criminal offence? What problems would ensue if we did this? Would everyone have equal difficulties if possessing knives in a public space was made a criminal offence?

Exercise 4

CASES II

5.10 ▶ Reread the appropriate parts of Chapters 4 and 5 before attempting the questions below. Remember to note which part of the judgment you are referring to when giving your answers. The answers for Section A are found in Appendix III.

Court of Appeal   *A*

In re B (A Child) (Wrongful Removal: Orders against Non-Parties)

[2014] EWCA Civ 843

2014 May 6;   Sir James Munby P, Black, Underhill LJJ   *B*
    June 20

*Children — Family proceedings — Evidence — Child wrongfully removed from
jurisdiction — Judge ordering 16-year-old half-brother to attend court, give
evidence and disclose documents — Penal notice attached to order — Judge
failing to balance half-brother's welfare interests as child against need to take
evidence from him — Whether order to be set aside — Judge finding evidence not*   *C*
*candid — Whether procedural irregularity in order for attendance at court under
threat of imprisonment rendering finding unjust*
*Children — Orders with respect to children — Penal notice — Order against child to
attend court and produce documents — Order endorsed with penal notice —
Whether wrong in principle to attach penal notice to order against child*
*Injunction — Jurisdiction to grant — Passport order — Child wrongfully removed
from jurisdiction — Judge making order endorsed with penal notice requiring*   *D*
*child's grandparents and minor half-brother to lodge passports with court —
Whether proper to make passport order for purpose of causing pressure to be
applied to child's mother to return child — Whether to be set aside — Whether
wrong in principle to attach penal notice to order against person too young to be
imprisoned or detained for contempt of court*

    The father of a child, who was a ward of court and who had been wrongfully   *E*
removed from the jurisdiction by her mother, sought her return under the
1980 Hague Convention on the Civil Aspects of International Child Abduction. In
those proceedings the judge, seeking to enlist the assistance of the wider family in
locating the child and her mother and ensuring the child's return, made an order,
endorsed with a penal notice, which, inter alia, (i) required the maternal
grandparents and the child's half-brother, who was 16 years old, to provide certain
information and to lodge their passports with the court, and (ii) the half-brother to   *F*
attend court on a specified date. The half-brother attended court on that date and
complied with the judge's order that he give evidence. The judge found that he had
not been completely candid with the court and made an order, again endorsed with a
penal notice, which, inter alia, required that the passports of the grandmother and the
half-brother remain lodged with the court, and that the half-brother attend the court
again and produce to the court records of telephone calls and other electronic
communications.   *G*
    On the half-brother's appeal—
    Held, allowing the appeal, (1) that it was not a permissible exercise of the court's
power to require a non-party, whether an adult or a child, who had no parental
responsibility or any other form of power or control over an abducted child to lodge
his or her passport with the court in order to coerce him or her to put pressure on the
abductor to return the child to the jurisdiction; and that, accordingly, the judge had
been wrong to order the half-brother and the grandparents to lodge their passports   *H*
with the court (post, paras 24, 33–35 44, 45).
    Dicta of Munby LJ in *In re HM (Vulnerable Adult: Abduction)* [2010] 2 FLR
1057, paras 36, 38 approved.
    In re B (Child Abduction: Wardship: Power to Detain) [1994] 2 FLR 479, CA
and *B v B (Injunction: Jurisdiction)* [1998] 1 WLR 329 considered.

A   (2) That it was wrong as a matter of principle to attach a penal notice where the
subject of the order had not reached the age at which he or she could be imprisoned
or detained for contempt of court, and so the judge had been wrong to endorse the
orders against the half-brother with a penal notice; that, since the judge had not
applied his mind to where the balance properly lay between the half-brother's welfare
interests as a child and the need to take evidence from him, the orders that he attend
court, give evidence and disclose the records of communications should not have
B   been made; that the order for disclosure was in any event not proportionate in that it
was manifestly too wide because there was no justification for making an order
extending beyond those records which were relevant to locating the whereabouts of
the abducted child and her mother; and that, since the making of the first order to
attend court which included an impermissible threat of imprisonment was a serious
procedural irregularity, the findings of lack of candidness made at that hearing were
unjust and could not stand (post, paras 36, 40, 41, 43, 44, 45).
C   In re W (Children) (Family Proceedings: Evidence) [2010] 1 WLR 701,
SC(E) applied.
       Decision of Judge Tyzack QC sitting as a judge of the Family Division reversed.

The following cases are referred to in the judgment of Sir James Munby P:

Anton Piller KG v Manufacturing Processes Ltd [1976] Ch 55; [1976] 2 WLR 162;
       [1976] 1 All ER 779, CA
D   B (Child Abduction: Wardship: Power to Detain), In re [1994] 2 FLR 479, CA
B v B (Injunction: Jurisdiction) [1998] 1 WLR 329; [1997] 3 All ER 258
Bayer AG v Winter [1986] 1 WLR 497; [1986] 1 All ER 733, CA
Bhura v Bhura [2012] EWHC 3633 (Fam); [2013] 2 FLR 44
Guzzardi v Italy (1980) 3 EHRR 333
HM (Vulnerable Adult: Abduction), In re [2010] EWHC 870 (Fam); [2010] 2 FLR
       1057
E   Harrow London Borough Council v G [2004] EWHC 17 (QB); [2004] NPC 4
J (A Minor) (Wardship), In re [1988] 1 FLR 65
MCA, In re (Long intervening) [2002] EWHC 611 (Admin/Fam); [2002] 2 FLR 274
Mareva Navigation Co Ltd v Canaria Armadora SA [1977] 1 Lloyd's Rep 368
S (Financial Provision: Non-Resident), In re [1996] 1 FCR 148
Thaha v Thaha [1987] 2 FLR 142
W (Children) (Family Proceedings: Evidence), In re [2010] UKSC 12; [2010] 1 WLR
F   701; [2010] PTSR 775; [2010] 2 All ER 418, SC(E)
Wookey v Wookey [1991] Fam 121; [1991] 3 WLR 135; [1991] 3 All ER 365, CA
Young v Young [2012] EWHC 138 (Fam); [2012] Fam 198; [2012] 3 WLR 266
ZH (Tanzania) v Secretary of State for the Home Department [2011] UKSC 4; [2011]
       2 AC 166; [2011] 2 WLR 148; [2011] 2 All ER 783, SC(E)

No additional cases were cited in argument.
G
The following additional cases, although not cited, were referred to in the skeleton
arguments:

Attorney General v Times Newspapers Ltd (No 3) [1992] 1 AC 191; [1991] 2 WLR
       994; [1991] 2 All ER 398, HL(E)
Campbell v MGN Ltd [2004] UKHL 22; [2004] 2 AC 457; [2004] 2 WLR 1232;
H   [2004] 2 All ER 995, HL(E)
George Wimpey UK Ltd v Tewkesbury Borough Council [2008] EWCA Civ 12;
       [2008] 1 WLR 1649; [2008] 3 All ER 859, CA
LC (Children) (Reunite International Child Abduction Centre intervening), In re
       [2014] UKSC 1; [2014] AC 1038; [2014] 2 WLR 124; [2014] 1 All ER 1181,
       SC(E)

R (AB) v Secretary of State for the Home Department [2013] EWHC 3453 (Admin);   A
    [2014] 2 CMLR 722
W (A Minor) (Medical Treatment: Court's Jurisdiction), In re [1993] Fam 64; [1992]
    3 WLR 758; [1992] 4 All ER 627, CA
X (A Minor) (Wardship: Jurisdiction), In re [1975] Fam 47; [1975] 2 WLR 335;
    [1975] 1 All ER 697, Latey J and CA

APPEAL from Judge Tyzack QC sitting as a judge of the Family Division   B
    In the course of proceedings under the 1980 Hague Convention on the Civil Aspects of International Child Abduction begun by the father of B, a nine-year-old ward of court who had been abducted by her mother and removed from the jurisdiction, on 27 February 2014 Judge Tyzack QC, sitting as a judge of the Family Division in the Exeter District Registry, ordered inter alia, that (i) the maternal grandparents and the mother's partner provide certain information and lodge their passports with the court, and (ii) B's elder   C half-brother, L, who had been born in May 1997, provide certain information, lodge his passport with the court and attend court on 28 March 2014, endorsing the order with a penal notice. On 28 March 2014 the judge, having heard L's evidence, found that he had not been completely candid with the court and ordered that (i) the passports of the maternal grandmother, the mother's partner and L remain lodged with the court; (ii) the applications by   D the maternal grandmother and L for the return of their passports be adjourned until 7 May 2014; (iii) L attend court on 7 May 2014; and (iv) L produce to the court forthwith all the records of telephone calls to and from his land line telephone and all records of any e-mails, texts or other electronic means of communication between 1 February 2014 and 7 May 2014. That order was endorsed with a penal notice in the same terms.
    By an appellant's notice filed on 11 April 2014 and pursuant to   E permission granted by the Court of Appeal (Black LJ) on 16 April 2014 L appealed seeking the discharge of those orders on the grounds that the judge had been wrong (1) to order his attendance at court, (2) to order that his passport remain lodged with the court, (3) to order disclosure of his communications, (4) to attach a penal notice to the orders made against him and (5) to conclude that he was not being candid in his evidence.   F
    On 2 May 2014 Sir James Munby P directed that the representatives (*Paul Storey* QC and *Anthony Ward* (instructed by *Cartridges, Exeter*)) for the children's guardian appointed under FPR r 16.4 for B, who had filed a skeleton argument supportive of the appeal, be excused attendance at the hearing.
    On 6 May 2014 at the conclusion of the hearing the court announced that the appeal would be allowed in respect of the passport order, for reasons to   G be given later.
    The facts are stated in the judgment of Sir James Munby P, post, paras 2–6.

    David Williams QC and *Alistair Perkins* (instructed by *Crosse + Crosse LLP, Exeter*) for L.   H
    The maternal grandparents in person.
    The father, mother and the mother's partner did not appear and were not represented.

    The court took time for consideration.

A   20 June 2014. The following judgments were handed down.

SIR JAMES MUNBY P

1   This is an appeal by a child against an order made by Judge
Tyzack QC, sitting as a judge of the Family Division in the Exeter District
Registry on 28 March 2014. It raises what are properly described as issues
of general public importance in respect of two matters: first, the powers of
B   the court to compel third parties without parental responsibility (or any
other form of power or control over the child) to take steps to secure the
return of an abducted child; and, second, the role of non-subject children in
such proceedings, the powers of the court in relation to them, and the basis
on which orders can properly be made against them having regard to
article 3.1 of the United Nations Convention on the Rights of the Child 1989
C   and article 8 of the European Convention for the Protection of Human
Rights and Fundamental Freedoms.

The background

2   The background facts can be very shortly summarised. Judge
Tyzack QC was concerned with a ward of court, a nine-year-old girl called
D   B, who had been abducted by her mother and removed from the
jurisdiction in order to avoid the consequences of orders previously made
by the court. In the course of proceedings begun by B's father, it became
appropriate for Judge Tyzack QC to enlist the assistance of the mother's
wider family in locating B and her mother and ensuring B's return to the
jurisdiction.

3   On 27 February 2014 Judge Tyzack QC made an order, endorsed with
E   a penal notice, which, so far as material, ordered the maternal grandparents
(Mr and Mrs S) and the mother's partner to provide certain information and
to lodge their passports with the court, and ordered B's elder half-brother, L,
born in May 1997 and therefore not yet 17 years old, to provide certain
information, to lodge his passport with the court and to attend court on
28 March 2014.

F   *The hearing before Judge Tyzack QC*

4   On 28 March 2014 L attended court. He was represented by
experienced family solicitors. In the position statement filed on his behalf,
his solicitors said:

> "The court is reminded of the guidelines issued by the Family Justice
G   Council in 2011 concerning children giving evidence in family
> proceedings. In deciding whether a child should give evidence, the court's
> principal objective should be achieving a fair trial. With that objective in
> mind the court should carry out a balancing exercise between, on the one
> part any possible advantages of the child's evidence and secondly any
> possible damage to the child's welfare of giving the evidence itself."

H   5   Despite that, Judge Tyzack QC required L to give evidence. In the
extempore judgment which he gave at the end of the hearing he said of L's
evidence:

> "I am not satisfied that he was fully and completely candid with the
> court . . . I would remind the family that if the court ever finds a serious

396
In re B (A Child) (CA)   [2015] 2 WLR
Sir James Munby P

A lack of candour it could amount to a contempt of court, and contempt in this jurisdiction is punishable by a maximum of two years' imprisonment. That is why the court requires absolute candour from everyone".

6 Judge Tyzack QC then made the order under appeal. So far as material, it ordered that the passports of the maternal grandmother, the mother's partner and L were to remain lodged with the court, that the B applications by the maternal grandmother and L for the return of their passports were adjourned until 7 May 2014, that L was to attend court on 7 May 2014, and that L was to:

"produce to the court forthwith all the records of telephone calls to and from his land line telephone and all records of any e-mails texts or other electronic means of communication [between 1 February 2014 and C 7 May 2014]."

The order was endorsed with a penal notice which, in the same terms as that endorsed on the previous order, stated:

"You have a right to ask the court to change or cancel the order but you must obey it unless the court does change or cancel it. You must obey the D instructions contained in this order. If you do not, you will be guilty of contempt and may be sent to prison."

Judge Tyzack QC's judgment

7 Judge Tyzack QC explained his reasons for making these orders in the following passages in his judgment, which require to be set out at length: E

"[Counsel], understandably, has applied for Mr and Mrs S's passports to be returned to them. It is said that they are caught in the middle, which I suppose in a sense they are. It is said that to retain their passports in court would be to punish them, which I suppose in a sense it does. They have a cruise booked, I think in May. They would like to go abroad to Ireland and to visit battlefields and cemeteries in France and Belgium. F Those things are normal, pleasurable activities which everybody in this country can, if they can afford it, obviously reasonably enjoy. But Mr and Mrs S, I am sorry to say, are caught up in a very unfortunate dispute and the court is not satisfied that they have fully and wholeheartedly co-operated in the court's endeavour to ensure that B is returned to the jurisdiction of England and Wales. I am going to adjourn G the application for Mr and Mrs S's passports to be returned because I would like to see, the court would like to see the extent to which Mrs S will now apply her mind, and maybe her husband's, to the essential task of putting persuasion/influence/pressure on [the mother] to return B to the jurisdiction of England and Wales. It is said by [counsel], in effect: 'What is the point of doing that because the mother has made up her mind and it is clear that she has made up her mind to stay where she is in Abu Dhabi H or Dubai?' That may be so. But that, in my judgment, should not prevent the court from seeking to rely upon, as the court is entitled to, to rely on Mr and Mrs S to put pressure and influence on their daughter to return B to the jurisdiction. So far, that has not been tried, and in my judgment

A   the time has come for it to be attempted. Their passports will remain in
     court.
         "Similar considerations apply to L. I appreciate that I am dealing with
     a 16-year-old boy even more tragically caught up in this mess. But I was
     very disappointed to hear the evidence which he gave . . .
         "I am not satisfied that the court has so far received absolute candour
B   from the wider family and absolute assistance and co-operation from
     them to influence their daughter or mother respectively to return. L's
     passport must remain in court. I adjourn his application until a later date,
     again, to see whether any appropriate pressure can be brought to bear on
     this mother to act lawfully."

The appeal

C
     8   On 15 April 2014 L filed an appellant's notice. The grounds of
     appeal, settled by leading counsel, were that Judge Tyzack QC was wrong
     (1) to order L's attendance at court on 7 May 2014, (2) to order that L's
     passport remain lodged with the court, (3) to order disclosure of L's
     communications, (4) to attach a penal notice to the orders made against L,
D   and (5) to conclude that L was not being candid in his evidence.
     9   The application for permission to appeal came before Black LJ as a
     paper application. On 16 April 2014 Black LJ gave L permission to appeal
     and directed a stay of the orders that he attend court on 7 May 2014 and
     produce records.
     10   The appeal came on before us for hearing on 6 May 2014. L was
E   represented by Mr David Williams QC and Mr Alistair Perkins. B's FPR
     r 16.4 guardian had filed a skeleton argument prepared by Mr Paul
     Storey QC and Mr Anthony Ward. As their skeleton argument was
     largely supportive of the appeal, I made a direction at their request on 2 May
     2014 dispensing with their attendance at the hearing. The mother was,
     unsurprisingly, neither present nor represented, nor was the mother's
     partner. The maternal grandparents were present but not represented.
F   11   The father also was neither present nor represented, but had written
     a letter to the court dated 22 April 2014 saying that he did not take a voice in
     the legal argument and was going to leave it to the court to decide what to
     do. He added: "Overall I think that the judge is doing his best in the interests
     of returning my daughter . . . back to this jurisdiction . . . My interest is for
     the safe return of my daughter". I can well understand that the father should
G   have adopted this stance.
     12   At the end of the hearing we announced that we were allowing the
     appeal in relation to ground 2—the retention of L's passport—while
     reserving our decision in relation to the other grounds of appeal.

Some general matters

H   13   Before addressing the various points raised by Mr Williams it is
     important to realise that nothing in this appeal puts in issue, and nothing we
     say is intended to throw any doubt on, the generality of the well established
     powers of the court when faced with the problem which confronted Judge
     Tyzack QC.

398
In re B (A Child) (CA)   [2015] 2 WLR
Sir James Munby P

14 In *In re HM (Vulnerable Adult: Abduction)* [2010] 2 FLR 1057,   *A*
para 36, I said:

"It has long been recognised that, quite apart from any statutory
jurisdiction (for example under section 33 of the Family Law Act 1986 or
section 50 of the Children Act 1989), the Family Division has an inherent
jurisdiction to make orders directed to third parties who there is reason to
believe may be able to provide information which may lead to the   *B*
location of a missing child. Thus orders can be made against public
authorities (for example, Her Majesty's Revenue and Customs, the
Benefits Agency, the Driver and Vehicle Licensing Agency, local
authorities or local education authorities, etc, etc) requiring them to
search their records with a view to informing the court whether they have
any record of the child or the child's parent or other carer. Similar orders
can be directed to telephone and other IT service providers, to banks and   *C*
other financial institutions, to airline and other travel service providers—
the latter with a view to finding out whether the missing child has in fact
left the jurisdiction and, if so, for what destination—and to relatives,
friends and associates of the abducting parent. In appropriate cases,
though this is usually confined to relatives, friends and associates, the
court can require the attendance at court to give oral evidence of anyone   *D*
who there is reason to believe may be able to provide relevant
information. Compliance with such orders can, where appropriate, be
enforced by endorsing the order with a penal notice and then, in the event
of non-compliance, issuing a bench warrant for the arrest and
compulsory production in court of the defaulter."

I see no reason to alter a word of that.   *E*

15 I added, at para 38:

"in aid of this jurisdiction the court can make a variety of orders
directed to the tipstaff, including, in addition to location, collection and
passport orders, an order authorising the tipstaff to enter private
residential property, if need be using force to open doors, with a view to
searching for, removing and taking into custody anything (for example, a   *F*
computer or a mobile phone, blackberry or other similar device) which
there is reason to believe may contain information throwing light on the
missing child's whereabouts . . ."

16 The reference there to passport orders will be noted. There is no
doubt that there are circumstances in which the High Court, in exercise of its
inherent jurisdiction, can properly make an order (what for shorthand I shall   *G*
refer to as a "passport order") requiring someone to lodge their passport
with the court or with some suitable custodian, for example the tipstaff or a
solicitor who has given the court an appropriate undertaking: see, for
example, *In re S (Financial Provision: Non-Resident)* [1996] 1 FCR 148, *B v
B (Injunction: Jurisdiction)* [1998] 1 WLR 329, *Young v Young* [2012] Fam
198 and *Bhura v Bhura* [2013] 2 FLR 44. The question is as to the ambit of
this power, in particular where, as here, the power is sought to be exercised   *H*
against a non-party.

17 It is against that background, none of which is in any way
controversial, that I turn to consider the issues formulated for our decision
by Mr Williams.

[2015] 2 WLR   In re B (A Child) (CA)
                                                         Sir James Munby P

A   *The passport order (ground 2)*

    18   I start with the second ground of appeal.

    19   There are two well recognised situations where the court may, and frequently does, make a passport order. One is aptly described in the words of Wilson J in *B v B (Injunction: Jurisdiction)* [1998] 1 WLR 329, 333:

B   "In the Family Division use is often made of a power to restrain a party from leaving the jurisdiction and to require the surrender of passports. Thus when, for example, a foreign plaintiff complains that the defendant has wrongfully abducted a child to England and Wales and seeks an order for the child's peremptory return under the Child Abduction and Custody Act 1985, it is normal to order at the outset that until the hearing the defendant do not leave England and Wales and do surrender his or her

C   passport. Such an order is made either under section 5 of the 1985 Act or pursuant to the court's inherent jurisdiction. Another example is where a foreign parent who might be disposed to misuse a period of contact in England in order to remove a child overseas is ordered in the exercise of the inherent jurisdiction to surrender his passport . . ."

That was not, of course, what Judge Tyzack QC was doing here.

D   20   The other situation is that described by Wilson J in *B v B*, at p 334:

"The jurisdiction exists where the other party has established a right to interlocutory relief, such as an *Anton Piller* order, which would otherwise be rendered nugatory. It exists where a hearing is shortly to take place, the efficacy of which would be frustrated by his absence."

E   21   Examples of such situations are to be found in *Bayer AG v Winter* [1986] 1 WLR 497, where a defendant was ordered not to leave the jurisdiction until he had complied with *Mareva* (see *Mareva Navigation Co Ltd v Canaria Armadora SA* [1977] 1 Lloyd's Rep 368) and *Anton Piller* (see *Anton Piller KG v Manufacturing Processes Ltd* [1976] Ch 55) orders requiring him to disclose information, *Thaha v Thaha* [1987] 2 FLR 142, where Wood J issued a writ ne exeat regno[1]* so as to detain a husband within

F   England for a few days until the hearing of a judgment summons which was to be issued against him for alleged arrears under orders for maintenance, *In re J (A Minor) (Wardship)* [1988] 1 FLR 65, where a mother was restrained from leaving the jurisdiction until she had undergone a blood test, and *In re S (Financial Provision: Non-Resident)* [1996] 1 FCR 148, 151, where Thorpe J said that there was power "to require a respondent . . . who is within this jurisdiction but who is not ordinarily resident within this

G   jurisdiction to surrender his passport pending an imminent fixture to determine interim financial provision".

    22   More recent examples include *Young v Young* [2012] Fam 198, where the respondent to financial remedy proceedings was restrained from leaving the jurisdiction pending the final hearing of the wife's claim in nine months' time. As Mostyn J said, and I agree, at para 26: "The power to

H   impound a passport pending the disposal of a financial remedy claim exists in principle in aid of all the court's procedures leading to the disposal of the proceedings."

    * *Reporter's note.* The superior figure in the text refers to the note which can be found at the end of Sir James Munby P's judgment on p 404.

23 This again, as will be appreciated, was not the basis on which Judge A
Tyzack QC made the passport orders in the present case.

24 Judge Tyzack QC was commendably clear and frank in explaining
why he was making the passport orders. It was to induce the maternal
grandmother and L to "apply [their minds] . . . to the essential task of
putting persuasion/influence/pressure on [the mother] to return [B] to
the jurisdiction", to "put pressure and influence on [her]". Was that a
permissible basis on which to make a passport order? In my judgment it was B
not. That follows from the decision of this court in *In re B (Child
Abduction: Wardship: Power to Detain)* [1994] 2 FLR 479.

25 In *In re B* the father took the children to Algeria without the
mother's consent. He returned to England without the children, who
remained with the grandparents in Algiers. Singer J concluded that the
father had deliberately sought to keep the children out of the jurisdiction for C
reasons unconnected with their welfare and doubted that the children would
be returned voluntarily to England. It was common ground, however, that
the father was not in contempt of court. Singer J ordered that the father be
detained by the tipstaff until the children were taken to the British Embassy
in Algiers. On the father's appeal this court discharged the order and
directed the father's release. D

26 It will be appreciated that Singer J's purpose in *In re B* was precisely
the same as Judge Tyzack QC's purpose in the present case, albeit that
Singer J had recourse to the more drastic method of incarceration.

27 Explaining why Singer J's order was impermissible, Butler-Sloss LJ
said, at pp 483–484:

> "The purpose of a bench warrant is to bring the person detained to E
> court and its purpose is effected as soon as he appears before the judge. At
> that moment he may or may not be in contempt of a court order. If he is
> not in contempt then in my view there is no power to detain him further.
> The direction of the court has been complied with and there is nothing
> before the court to enable the further power of detention to be invoked. If
> the person is prima facie guilty of contempt but the proceedings are part
> heard and are continuing, I can see no reason, in certain circumstances, F
> not to detain him pending the conclusion of the case if the court is
> satisfied that he will not voluntarily attend on the next hearing day. The
> purpose is to secure the attendance of the alleged contemnor for the next
> court hearing. *There is no precedent for detaining a party or a witness at
> the end of the hearing in order to compel another to comply with a court
> order.*" (Emphasis added.) G

She added: "The heart-rending emotions of a child abduction case do not
take it outside the proper exercise of the court's powers."

28 Hobhouse LJ gave judgment to the same effect, at pp 485–486:

> "the purpose of detaining the father was to bring pressure to bear upon
> and influence the conduct of the grandparents in Algeria. They were
> being told, in effect, your son is being held in prison in London and he will H
> not be released until you return the grandchildren. It was thus an exercise
> in coercion whereby an individual was being deprived of his liberty so as
> to coerce others into doing what the court wishes. In my judgment,
> however laudable the motives or worthy the objective, this is not a power

A   which is part of the law of England; nor should it form part of any civilised system of law."

29   The only point of difference between that case and this is that whereas in *In re B (Child Abduction: Wardship: Power to Detain)* [1994] 2 FLR 479 the coercive method applied by the judge was incarceration, in this case it was a passport order. Now there are, of course, in certain

B   respects very great differences between the two forms of order. In the one case the hapless witness is confined to a prison cell; in the other he is confined to the United Kingdom—islands, as Mostyn J pointed out in *Young v Young* [2012] Fam 198, para 6, very much larger than the island to which the Mafioso in *Guzzardi v Italy* (1980) 3 EHRR 333 had been confined. Moreover, in the one case he is deprived of his liberty, thus engaging article 5

C   of the Convention; in the other what is involved is no more than an interference with his liberty of movement and freedom to leave the country, engaging article 2 of Protocol 4 to the Convention (which, it may be noted, is not binding on the United Kingdom).

30   In *B v B (Injunction: Jurisdiction)* [1998] 1 WLR 329, 334 Wilson J, referring to a submission put to him by counsel in that case, Mr Nicholas Mostyn, said: "Mr Mostyn suggests that a restraint upon leaving England

D   and Wales is wholly unlike imprisonment. I disagree."

31   In *Young v Young* [2012] Fam 198, para 6 Mostyn J commented in relation to Wilson J's observation "that was decided before the advent of the Human Rights Act 1998 and without consideration of the Strasbourg jurisprudence." That no doubt is so, and was highly material in the context of the point Mostyn J was considering, namely the applicability of article 5

E   of the Convention in the case before him.

32   But Wilson J's words surely suggest, what a reading of his judgment as a whole indicates, that his observation was not directed to the Strasbourg distinction between a deprivation of liberty and an interference with liberty of movement, but rather to a different and for present purposes much more significant point; namely, that either form of coercive sanction is equally outside the proper ambit of the court's powers as a matter of domestic law.

F   For immediately after the words I have just quoted, Wilson J cited these words of Hobhouse LJ in *In re B (Child Abduction: Wardship: Power to Detain)* [1994] 2 FLR 479, 488:

"The use of ancillary powers which have the practical effect of restricting the liberty, or freedom of movement of an individual is recognised in the granting of injunctions, now under section 37 of the

G   Supreme Court Act 1981 . . . There is an obvious difference in kind between an injunction and the arrest or physical detention of an individual, but such orders are analogous and illustrate the proper use of an ancillary power although it prima facie infringes the personal rights of the individual involved.

"Where a power of arrest or detention has been recognised other than

H   as part of a punitive jurisdiction, it is ancillary to the exercise of another power of the court and is legitimate because it is necessary to the implementation of the order of the court."

33   In my judgment it is clear that, for this purpose, neither Hobhouse LJ nor Wilson J saw any material difference between a coercive order where the

402
In re B (A Child) (CA)   [2015] 2 WLR
Sir James Munby P

coercive method used is incarceration and a coercive order where the   A
coercive method used is a passport order. Each is equally outside the proper
ambit of the court's powers. Mr Williams referred in this context to
Sippenhaft*. The point was well made: cf *In re MCA (Long intervening)*
[2002] 2 FLR 274, para 190.

34   It follows that Mr Williams succeeds on this ground of appeal.

35   It will be appreciated that none of this has anything to do with the   B
fact that, in law, L is a child. Judge Tyzack QC was wrong to make a
passport order in relation to L. He was equally wrong, and for precisely the
same reasons, to make passport orders in relation to the maternal
grandparents. The only difference between the two cases is that L has
appealed, whereas the maternal grandparents have not. Their remedy, in the
first instance, is a renewed application to Judge Tyzack QC. It was for this
reason that, on this point, we announced our decision at the conclusion of   C
the hearing so that Judge Tyzack QC would be aware of the outcome when
the matter came back before him the following day.

The penal notice (ground 4)

36   I can deal with this point very shortly. At the relevant time L was not
yet 17 years old. He could therefore not be imprisoned or detained for   D
contempt. In these circumstances it was simply wrong as a matter of
principle to attach to the order a penal notice in the form used by Judge
Tyzack QC: see *Wookey v Wookey* [1991] Fam 121, and *Harrow London
Borough Council v G* [2004] EWHC 17 (QB); [2004] NPC 4. On this short
ground the appeal on this point must be allowed.

                                                                          E
The order to attend court (ground 1)

37   Mr Williams placed the main weight of his argument, and in my
judgment rightly so, on the decision of the Supreme Court in *In re
W (Children) (Family Proceedings: Evidence)* [2010] 1 WLR 701. He
bolstered his argument with reference to what the Supreme Court has more
recently said in *ZH (Tanzania) v Secretary of State for the Home   F
Department* [2011] 2 AC 166, about article 3.1 of the United Nations
Convention on the Rights of the Child 1989. While I can quite understand
why he did so, I think we can properly proceed on a narrower front, for
compliance with the learning in *In re W (Children)* will, in my judgment,
meet whatever obligations arise under article 3.1.

38   Mr Williams submits that Judge Tyzack QC never embarked on the
evaluation, required by *In re W (Children)*, of where the balance properly   G
lay between, on the one hand, the need to take evidence from L and, on the
other hand, L's welfare interests. He submits that Judge Tyzack QC never
evaluated, as he should have, the impact on L's article 8 rights of being
compelled to give evidence: both his article 8 right to family life (his
relationship with his mother, likely to be imperilled if he was compelled to
"grass" on her) and his right to private life (his telephone and e-mail
communications). He submits that if satisfied that the balance fell in favour   H
of requiring L to provide information, Judge Tyzack QC should have gone
on to consider *how* that ought to be achieved, whether for example a

* *Reporter's note.* Sippenhaft means kin liability for a crime.

A direction for the filing of a written statement or for a video interview would have sufficed.

39 Mr Williams submits that Judge Tyzack QC failed to undertake this exercise adequately, if at all. He says that a proper application of the *In re W (Children)* approach required careful attention to the emotional impact on L of being forced to give evidence which was likely to place him in conflict with his mother and sister and of being cross-examined on behalf of B a man who he said had behaved abusively to his mother, to him and to his sister.

40 In my judgment, Mr Williams succeeds on this ground of appeal. There is nothing in either the transcript of the proceedings or the judgment to suggest that Judge Tyzack QC ever really applied his mind to the matters which *In re W (Children)* required to be considered. It is true, and in justice C to Judge Tyzack QC I make clear, that he did not have the benefit of the much fuller argument which Mr Williams has addressed to us. But the point had been flagged up in the position statement filed on L's behalf and the fact is that the judge simply did not engage with it in any meaningful way. What the outcome would have been if he had undertaken an appropriate *In re W (Children)* analysis it is impossible to say. For all I know, Judge D Tyzack QC might have concluded that the balance came down on the side of requiring L to give evidence. That, however, is speculation, and speculation is not a proper basis for deciding an appeal. L is entitled to have this part of the order set aside.

The order for disclosure (ground 3)

E 41 Much the same arguments apply here as in relation to the previous ground of appeal. Judge Tyzack QC should have evaluated whether requiring L to disclose this material was proportionate. He did not. Quite apart from that, the order is manifestly too wide in the circumstances of this case. It covers "all" records of the types specified, whereas on any footing there was no justification here (I say nothing about any other case) for making an order extending beyond those records which were relevant to F locating the whereabouts of B and her mother. That suffices in my judgment to dispose of the appeal in L's favour. Mr Williams submits that in any event, to the extent that the order is in the nature of a mandatory injunction it should not have been made against a child: *Harrow London Borough Council v G* [2004] EWHC 17 (QB). That is probably correct, but we do not need to decide the point and I prefer not to.

G *The finding in relation to L's evidence (ground 5)*

42 Mr Williams submits, for the same reasons as he deploys in relation to ground 1, that the earlier order dated 27 February 2014 which led to L attending court on 28 March 2014, and moreover attending under an impermissible threat of imprisonment if he did not (see ground 4), was wrong and should not have been made. This, he says, was a serious H procedural irregularity. He submits that Judge Tyzack QC's finding against L that he had not been candid cannot stand. The procedural irregularity made the finding unjust. Moreover, he submits, Judge Tyzack QC failed to make any allowance for the circumstances in arriving at his adverse finding against L.

404
In re B (A Child) (CA)   **[2015] 2 WLR**
Sir James Munby P

A

43   I confess that on this point my mind has wavered, both during
the hearing of the appeal and since. I have on balance concluded that
Mr Williams is right. I would therefore allow the appeal on this ground as
well.

Note

1. As Wilson J pointed out in *B v B (Injunction: Restraint on Leaving Jurisdiction)*
[1998] 1 WLR 329, 334, the use of the writ ne exeat regno was inapt at that stage in
the proceedings, though the order was entirely permissible under section 37(1) of the
Supreme Court Act 1981 (now the Senior Courts Act 1981).

B

BLACK LJ
   44   I agree.

UNDERHILL LJ
   45   I agree.

C

Appeal allowed.

JEANETTE BURN, *Barrister*

D

Section A

1. In what courts was this case heard?
2. What is a "passport order"?
3a. Is it lawful to detain someone in prison so as to make someone else obey a court order?
3b. What is your authority for your answer?
4. The passport order made against L did not involve imprisoning him. Why was consideration of a court's power to imprison someone relevant to deciding whether or not the court could lawfully make a passport order against L?
5. In the original hearing the judge considered the need to take evidence from L. What else ought he to have considered and why?

Section B

6. Black LJ and Underhill LJ simply agree with the judgement of Munby P. Why not have a single judge in court?
7. Write a short statement giving the ratio in this case.
8. a.) What are the reasons for and against making children like L give evidence in this kind of case?
   b.) Should the courts try to make children like L put pressure on their mothers to obey court orders?
9. The parties to this case are anonymised. Why is that so? Are there any disadvantages to annoymising parties to a case?

Legal Reasoning in Judgments

THE HIERARCHY OF PRECEDENT

As we noted in Chapter 1 there is a hierarchy of courts with respect to precedents. Judgements of ▶ 6.1
the Supreme Court are binding on all courts below it. However, because of a 1960 House of Lords
Practice Statement, judgements of the Supreme Court are not binding on itself. The Supreme
Court will normally follow its own previous judgements in order to ensure consistency and predictability in the operation of the legal system but it is not legally obliged to do so. However, it may be
possible to persuade the court that social circumstances have changed so that what it previously
held to be the law is no longer good law. Equally it may be possible to persuade the court that its
previous judgement was simply badly reasoned.

Judgements of the Court of Appeal, the court below the Supreme Court, are not binding on
the Supreme Court. They are binding on all courts below the Court of Appeal. The Court of Appeal
is said normally to be bound by its own previous decisions but there are a considerable and increasing number of exceptions to this general rule. In the past several judges in the Court of Appeal have
argued that the Court of Appeal should not be bound by its own previous decisions. They have suggested that the reasons for allowing the House of Lords to depart from its own previous decisions
are equally valid when applied to the Court of Appeal. In addition to this in practice in many areas
of law people cannot afford to take their cases to the Supreme Court; requiring the Court of Appeal
to follow its own previous decisions therefore means that law cannot develop quickly enough in
the light of changing social circumstances. The court below the Court of Appeal is the High Court.
Decisions of the High Court do not bind the Court of Appeal or the Supreme Court. They do bind
all courts below the High Court. Decisions of the High Court, however, do not bind the High Court
itself.

None of the courts below the High Court create precedents. Whilst their decisions are binding
on the parties to the case they do not create rules of law that are binding on the courts in new cases.

RATIO AND OBITER

Even when a previous case is binding within the hierarchy of the courts, different parts of the judg- ▶ 6.2
ment have to be treated in different ways. Lawyers distinguish two parts of a judgment: (a) the
ratio decidendi and (b) that which is *obiter dicta* (*obiter dictum* in the singular). These two terms,
ratio decidendi and obiter dicta, are commonly shortened to *ratio* and *obiter*. Put most simply, the
ratio in a judgement is that part of reasoning in the judgment which is necessary in order to reach
the conclusion that the judge arrived at. It is this that is *binding* on other courts in the hierarchy.
Obiter dicta is a term that describes the remainder of the judgment. Examples of things that will
usually be obiter dictum include reflections in a judgement on the historical development of a

	Importance in Precedence
Supreme Court (formerly House of Lords)	Binds courts below but not itself
Court of Appeal	Binds courts below and normally binds itself
High Court	Binds courts below but not itself
Crown Court	Binds no-one
County Court	Binds no-one

particular area of law or consideration of what decision the court would have made if the facts of the case had been different. Remarks in a judgement that are obiter are not binding on future courts. Thus, for example, in principle a magistrates' court could choose not to follow parts of a judgement from the Supreme Court that were merely obiter dicta, even though the Supreme Court is higher in the hier- archy of courts. However things that are obiter dicta in a judgement cannot simply be ignored; they are said to be *persuasive*. In the absence of a binding ratio the court may be influenced by obiter, particularly if that obiter is something that was said in a judgement in one of the higher courts within the legal system such as the Supreme Court or the Court of Appeal.

The basic distinction between ratio and obiter is clear enough. Three things are, however, more difficult. The first is deciding what the ratio of any particular case in fact is. The second is understanding exactly what is meant by saying that obiter is persuasive. The third is deciding to what degree, if at all, the judges actually follow the rules about ratio and obiter when they are arriving at their judgements. All these matters are areas of considerable controversy.

Judges do not, in their own judgements, say which part of the judgement is ratio and which part is obiter. The reader has to decide what the ratio is for themselves. However the decision is not simply a subjective one. What *you* are trying to do is to predict what future *courts* will say the ratio of a past case is. If you can do this then you can predict what the courts will think the case tells them to do. In turn if you can do this you have more chance of saying what judgements future courts will produce. Because this is what you are trying to do it does not matter what you think the ratio is. If your view differs from that of the courts you will not know what the courts are going to do. You need to know what the courts will think. Equally, however, you do not know which judge will be deciding a case in the future. Thus what you are trying to do is to predict what an unknown judge in the future decides is the ratio of a past case. If you are to do this then it would seem that there have to be rules for determining the ratio that both you and the judge follow. If you use the same rules as the judge, and if you both use them correctly, you will arrive at the same answer.

Whilst there is general agreement between many academics and judges about the broad nature of the rules that surround the notions of ratio and obiter there is much disagreement about the detail. One starting point, however, is the observation that legal reasoning in the English courts is usually pragmatic in its nature. This means that the courts do not start with some general statement of legal principle but, instead, tend to begin with the facts of the case before them and then try to say what legal rules apply to those facts. Of course not all the facts in a case are important. The fact that the contract was made on a Friday will not usually matter. Whether or not somebody who is alleged to have conducted an assault was wearing a blue tracksuit or a red one might matter in terms of identifying the culprit but it will not affect how legal rules are applied. Legal reasoning thus begins with the facts of the case but it begins only with what some people have called the *material* facts of the case. These facts are, very roughly, the facts that are central to the law in the case. The question then is how do we determine what are the material facts of a case. What rules help us decide?

The facts of the case are the facts stated in, or sometimes to be implied from, the judgement. It does not matter if the judge is plainly mistaken about those facts. If a judge makes a mistake about the facts of a case that might mean that the case will be taken to a higher appellate court. However, for the purpose of determining the legal rules that flow from the judgement, the facts are as the judge states them. If the judge says that a fact is material then it is so. Judges rarely do this. They usually talk about the facts in the case in their judgements but they often include many that are not material. There are certain presumptions about which are and which are not material facts. Facts about where something happened, when it happened and who it happened to, for example, are rarely material facts. However, the rules run out when it comes to deciding exactly what is a material fact and what is not. A material fact is a fact that is central to the reasoning of the case, central to the line of argument that leads to the conclusion that the judge reached, but it is difficult to be more precise than that. The ratio is then the rule that arises as the result of the judge's reasoning about these material facts.

A ratio in a previous case only binds a court if it is addressing the same legal issue that arises in the new case. The fact that the Supreme Court has decided something about the law of murder will not usually matter if the current case before the court, whichever court it is, is about theft. In order to decide whether there is a binding precedent for a new case before the court it is necessary first to decide what the ratio of a previous case is and then to decide whether or not the previous case and the present case are sufficiently analogous. In deciding this, the notion of material facts is again said to be useful. Are the material facts in the two cases the same or similar? If so there will be a binding precedent. Deciding whether or not a previous case is sufficiently analogous with a new one so as to make a binding precedent is, in itself, a difficult task. Judges will sometimes draw a distinction, sometimes a very fine distinction, between two apparently similar cases. They are then said to *distinguish* the previous case.

All parts of a judgement need to be read because even obiter, although not binding, are persuasive. However, what persuasive means in this context is not entirely clear. "Persuasive" in ordinary conversation means something like "provides good reasons". However persuasive in the context of legal reasoning seems to mean something rather different. The higher the court the dicta comes from the more persuasive it is taken to be. This could be for several reasons. First higher courts are appellate courts. Lower courts might find their judgements taken on appeal to those higher courts. Dicta from the higher courts might indicate how the higher courts will treat a particular issue when it becomes central to a case before it. Secondly the higher the court, in principle, generally the better and more experienced the judges should be. Obiter from such judges ought to have some kind of authority which stems from the knowledge of those who produce the dicta. Neither argument, however, is entirely convincing. Many, perhaps most, cases are not appealed even when they could be because of pressure of time or money. Why, then should lower courts worry about the prospect of appeal? More importantly, if cases are appealed, the appellate courts may change their minds about an issue, particularly when it becomes central to the trial and the argument that counsel puts forward. Obiter remarks are a far from perfect guide to what the authors of those dicta will decide in the future. Equally, even experienced judges make mistakes. A ratio that is clearly incorrectly argued is nevertheless a binding ratio. Is incorrectly argued obiter from a higher court still "persuasive"? It seems that it is but, then, what the word persuasive means is a little mysterious.

Everyone would accept that when the higher courts pass judgements they refer to previous cases. There are very few judgements of any length in the law reports that do not have copious references to past judgements. The traditional view is that the rules described above in chapter one about the hierarchy of the courts and the distinction between ratio and obiter described above in this chapter are sufficiently clear and sufficiently rigid so as to mean that most judicial decisions can be predicted before they are made. It is not just that there are legal rules. There are also rules and principles about how judges make law by referring to past cases and how they interpret statutes. Judges are bound by them. Thus, if you know what they are and if you read enough previous judgements, on most occasions, because of this, you will know what the court is going to decide. However many academics now view such a statement with some scepticism.

We have seen above that, even in a very elementary explanation of the notion of precedent, there are gaps in the rules that surround the notions of ratio and obiter. At the points where these gaps exist, the rules do not tell judges what they must decide. Choice or discretion is given to the judiciary. How large these gaps are is a matter for debate. However they are certainly there. When thinking about how precedent works we also need to take account of the fact that judges make many decisions each year. They make far more than they did in the past. This has created a great mass of previous judgements often offering a range of alternative views about the law in any one area. In trying to decide which precedents are applicable, in distinguishing or not distinguishing previous cases, the judiciary are also faced with choices. Here again the rules that are said to guide them might be thought to be vague and imprecise. Finally many modern judges and an even greater number of academics believe that some judicial decisions involve, at least in part, consideration of policy issues. Legal decisions sometimes involve decisions about things other than legal rules. Rules about ratio, obiter and the hierarchy of the courts are of little assistance in these instances. Here again judges are faced with discretion and choice.

To suggest that the traditional rules of precedent are of limited assistance in explaining how judges reach their decisions is not to argue that judicial behaviour is wholly unpredictable. Equally

such a suggestion does not involve arguing that judicial decisions are mere personal whims or that
cases that are found in the law reports are inconsequential when looking at legal rules. Instead it is to argue that judicial use of past cases is often more subtle than has previously been thought. Sometimes judges do talk about ratio and obiter in their judgements in the way described above. However this is infrequent. Even when they do not overtly refer to the rules above they may still be following them. Nevertheless what may be as important is a need that judges feel to justify their new decisions by references to what other judges have previously decided. In doing this they are seeking to show that their decisions are in keeping with the spirit of the legal system; they are not just their own individual preferences for what the law ought to be. This constrains what they can decide. Previous case law contains a wealth of views about the law but it does push thought in particular directions and thus makes some decisions more likely than others.

The legislature plainly makes new legal rules. The traditional notion is that common law rules do not alter to meet the requirements of society (or "public opinion"); it is the role of the legislator to remedy this through statutory intervention with specific legislation, and not for the judges to create new rules. The legislature makes law; the judiciary merely apply it. However, many academics and some judges would now argue that the judiciary sometimes do more than simply apply existing law; that in looking for rules of law in previous cases the judiciary subtly change the rules, consciously or otherwise, so that they produce the conclusions that they seek. If this is correct the judiciary are, in this sense, just as much legislators as Parliament.

FURTHER READING

F. Cownie, A. Bradney and M. Burton, *English Legal System in Context,* 6th edn, Oxford University ▶ 6.3
Press, (2013), Chapter 5.
R. Cross and J. Harris, *Precedent in English Law,* 4th edn, Oxford University Press, (1991).
P. Goodrich, *Reading the Law: Critical Introduction to Legal Method and Techniques*, WileyBlackwell, (1986), particularly Chapter 6.

▶ 7
Statutory Interpretation

JUDGES AND STATUTES

7.1 ▶ The traditional view, which has been accepted since at least the nineteenth century, is that the judiciary are bound by and, legally, must apply legislation, whether it is primary legislation or secondary legislation, no matter what its content. This is known as the *doctrine of parliamentary sovereignty*. This principle has the advantage that it separates clearly the role of the legislature, which is democratically elected to pass laws, and the judiciary, whose job it is to use their technical expertise to apply those laws. This, in turn, relates to a political concept, known as *the separation of powers*, under which the legislature, the executive and the judiciary have different but complementary roles in the political running of the country.

When the doctrine of parliamentary sovereignty is applied to the job of the judiciary one potential problem with this approach to the judicial role is that a statute might be passed that does something that is fundamentally objectionable. It might, for example, take away part of the population's right of access to the courts. A political principle, known as *the rule of law,* says, amongst other things, that everybody should be subject to the law and that the law should treat people equally. Many people see this as being fundamental to the maintenance of a liberal democracy. However the doctrine of parliamentary sovereignty in its traditional form does not guarantee that there will be adherence to the rule of law. If Parliament passes a statute saying all people with red hair will no longer have the right to vote the doctrine of parliamentary sovereignty says that the judges should enforce that law. Given that there is no written constitution for the UK, guaranteeing people's rights, this does not seem to be entirely satisfactory.

Not everyone is now convinced that, if a statute was passed that contravened the rule of law, judges should necessarily apply it. Some judges have argued that, at the very least, if a statute takes away the fundamental rights of the population as a whole, or a group of people in the country, it has to do so in very clear language before it could be enforced in the courts. Parliament has to make it plain that they intend to deny people rights that morally the population might think that they ought to have. The majority of people, including the majority of judges, still adhere to the traditional notion of parliamentary sovereignty. However, some people, including some judges, think this principle is too simplistic for the modern era. There should be some limits to what legislation Parliament can pass and expect the judiciary to apply. How we decide what those limits are is a difficult matter. Nevertheless we ought to agree that judges should not enforce every conceivable statute. However, even people who take this view think that judges should normally apply primary or secondary legislation whatever it says, even if, privately, they disapprove of its content.

Even if you do take the view that judges should always apply legislation you have to accept that sometimes an Act or piece of delegated legislation may be unclear or ambiguous. In some cases the difficulty will be resolved by applying one of the general Interpretation Acts. These are Acts that give a definition of words commonly found in legislation. Thus, for example, one Interpretation Act, the Interpretation Act 1978, says that where a piece of legislation uses the word "he" or "she" this should be taken to mean "he or she" unless it is plain from the context that this should not be so. Some Acts have their own interpretation section, in which certain important words or phrases used in the Act are defined. However, if a difficulty cannot be resolved by such an Act or section, if the ambiguity or lack of clarity remains, it is for the judiciary to decide what the legislation means.

THE PRINCIPLES OF STATUTORY INTERPRETATION

In order to discover the way in which legislation should be applied, the judges have developed a complex network of principles for statutory interpretation, which are designed to assist in the proper application of the law. Although these principles are often called rules they are not rules in the strictest of senses. If you drive above 70 miles per hour, if caught and convicted, you will be punished. The rule is clear and when it is to be applied is clear. The principles of statutory interpretation are much more unclear. There is no definitive source for what any one of these principles actually says. When they should be applied is also a matter of constant debate. This is not to say that they have no substance at all. Judges sometimes talk about them explicitly when they are passing judgment. They are part of the language which many people use when they analyse what judges do. However some people would argue that these so-called principles cloak, in part or whole, what judges do when they interpret statutes. When we look at statutory interpretation, they would argue, we should put the emphasis on the word "interpretation". Judges may talk about these principles of statutory interpretation in their judgments, they would suggest, but what judges actually do is to make personal choices about how to read a statute. Their individual choices are influenced by things like their education and the legal culture in which they work. They are not simply personal whims. For this reason their choices are to some degree predictable. However, for some people, judicial decisions about how to interpret a statute are not really influenced by the principles of statutory interpretation discussed below.

⬤ 7.2

The traditional starting point for statutory interpretation is *the literal rule*. The judiciary ought to look at the statute and apply its words literally. This principle accords with the traditional doctrine of parliamentary sovereignty. Parliament decided what the law should be and expressed their wishes through the language of the statute. The courts must interpret those words literally. However, although the literal rule seems to offer an easy solution to the problem of statutory interpretation, in practice its application raises many difficulties. First words often, and perhaps even usually, have a number of different meanings. We may not be familiar with all of these meanings. In ordinary conversation we use only a limited range of meanings. However, if you look at the 20 volumes of the Oxford English Dictionary, the complexity of the English language immediately becomes apparent. It is also the case that sometimes words have ordinary, everyday meanings and also technical meanings. Equally words are usually read as parts of phrases or sentences. Rules of grammar tell us how to read such groupings but rules of grammar are not precise and are subject to debate.

On the face of it the literal rule seems to take away choice from the judiciary when they interpret legislation. They should just follow the words that Parliament used. But in many instances, and some would argue in almost all instances, language gives us a choice of meanings, with there being more than one literal meaning that could be followed. We have to choose between meanings, to choose between ordinary and technical meanings or to decide which rules of grammar apply to the construction of the particular phrase in the statute before us.

There is no doubt that in the past the literal rule had substantial support from the judiciary. They cited the literal rule as a reason for their judgments. In doing so they denied that they exercised any discretion when they passed judgment. However whether it actually adequately described their practices is another matter. In the present day both most academics and judges, because they acknowledge the complexities of language, will be uncomfortable with the idea that the literal rule will usually be of much assistance in deciding how to interpret a statutory provision. It may be used sometimes but usually it is too simplistic a principle to help when trying to work out what a statute means.

The second principle of statutory interpretation that can be used is *the golden rule* or *the purposive approach*. Following this approach the courts should look at a statute as a whole. Where there is more than one meaning that could be put to a particular provision, and where one of those meanings would lead to an "absurdity or inconvenience" in the context of the interpretation of the statute taken as a whole, then the courts should choose the other meaning, even if grammatically it seems to be the less appropriate choice. It is argued that such an approach, even when it involves not following the literal meaning of the words chosen by Parliament, complies with the traditional notion of parliamentary sovereignty because it could not have been Parliament's intention to write a statute that contained a clear absurdity. In more modern language, when interpreting statutes courts ought to have an eye to the purpose of that statute. This approach does acknowledge that judges play a role in creating law, even when they are interpreting legislation, because they are making choices about what meanings they should apply. However, following this approach, their choice is constrained by the idea that they are making choices that would best fit with what must have been the intention of Parliament when they passed the statute. The choices they make are not personal decisions about what policy they think ought to underlie the law. Moreover the judges are still following the language of the statute.

The final broad principle that is applied to statutory interpretation is *the mischief rule*. The mischief rule still adheres to the traditional notion of parliamentary sovereignty. However the mischief rule says that sometimes Parliament's choice of language in a statute is so poor that any sensible interpretation of the statutory provisions as they have been laid down will not lead to the desired change in the law that was clearly the intention of Parliament. In such cases, following the mischief rule, the courts may be forced to read a statute as though it said something other than what it actually says so as to reach the result that Parliament intended. The statute says X but the courts will read it as though it says Y. One problem in applying this principle lies in knowing how the courts will be sure what the intention of Parliament with respect to an individual statute was. Since the 1990s the courts have increasingly looked to Hansard, the record of what is said in Parliament, to seek to ascertain the intention of statutes. As with the previous principle of statutory interpretation there is no straightforward clash between this principle and the traditional notion of parliamentary sovereignty. The courts are still said to be following the intention of Parliament. However this principle does give the courts considerable discretionary powers to create what is in effect new statutory language. Some will question how far such choices really reflect the court's knowledge of what Parliament actually intended, notwithstanding the contrary evidence of the language they used.

One final important influence on statutory interpretation is the Human Rights Act 1998. The 1998 Act incorporated many of the rights found in the European Convention on Human Rights into domestic law meaning that, in addition to the right that everyone has to take a case to the European Court of Human Rights, they are now enforceable within the domestic courts. When the courts are interpreting a statute they are now required, under the Human Rights Act, to inter- pret a statute, "so far as possible", so that it accords with the Convention rights. Once again this requirement does not contradict the traditional notion of parliamentary sovereignty. The courts must look at the language of a statute and see whether it can be interpreted in a way that is in keeping with the Convention. This might involve an interpretation that is more strained than it otherwise would be. However Parliament, in the 1998 Act, has told them that is what they should do. Moreover, although there can be a strained interpretation of a statutory provision, the courts must still follow the language of the statute. Where it is not possible to interpret a statute so that it accords with Convention rights the courts can issue a *declaration of incompatibility*. Where this has been done that statute is still valid law but Parliament and others have been alerted to the fact that the provisions of a statute are incompatible with people's Convention rights. In practice Parliament will amend the legislation so that it does not breach people's Convention rights, although this may take some time, but it is not legally bound to do this.

FURTHER READING

F. Cownie, A. Bradney and M. Burton, *English Legal System in Context*, 6th edn, Oxford University Press, (2013), Chapter 6.   ▶ 7.3

R. Cross, J. Bell and G. Engle, *Cross: Statutory Interpretation*, 3rd edn, Oxford University Press, (1995).

P. Goodrich, *Reading the Law: Critical Introduction to Legal Method and Techniques*, Wiley Blackwell, (1986), particularly Chapter 4.

▶ 8
Reading research materials

8.1 ▶ Chapter 4 explained that one way to answer questions about law was to use research methods taken from the social sciences and humanities. Because this kind of research is the only way in which some questions about law can be answered, it is important that those interested in law can understand it.

In order to understand research into law you have to understand how and why it is written in the particular way that it is. Once you can understand the structure of the material, you will be able to see whether or not it helps to answer the questions in which you are interested.

Haphazard approaches to research are likely to be unsuccessful, the information gathered being too unrepresentative of the world at large and, therefore, too inaccurate for any conclusions to be drawn safely. Good research is done systematically. Research methods are highly developed. There are three sources of information about how and why the law operates: records, people and activities. There are also three principal methods used in socio-legal research. The researcher may read records, interview people (or send questionnaires), or observe activities.

RECORD READING

8.2 ▶ Information is recorded for a wide range of purposes; the information contained depends on the primary purpose of the recording, which is not usually research. For example: applicants in legal proceedings must file an application—the information required depends on the nature of the case; the police must record specific details when people are arrested or detained in custody; courts keep records of each case so they can manage individual cases. Organisations of all sorts keep adminis-trative data about the work they do to establish the productivity of staff, the use of other resources and plan their services. Both case and administrative data can provide the basis for research about aspects of the operation of law.

The researcher has to collect the information required by extracting it from existing records or obtaining access to a database. All the information which could be useful for a particular study may not be available—records may not be complete and the database may not include all the required information.

INTERVIEWS AND QUESTIONNAIRES

8.3 ▶ Interviews are conducted in person, either face-to-face or by telephone. Questionnaires are given, sent or made available via the web for the respondents to complete. It is important, in so far as is possible, to ask the same questions in the same way each time so as to get comparable information. Questions may be "open", allowing the respondent to reply in his or her own words, or be "closed", requiring selection of the answer from a choice given by the interviewer. The style and wording of the question is selected to fit the data sought. Whatever the questions, the interview must be recorded. This may be done by using a digital recorder or by the interviewer noting the replies. Interviews are most useful for finding out what reasons people have for what they have done and for exploring their feelings. If questions are asked about the future, the answers can only indicate what respondents currently think they would do. It has also been established that recollection of past events may be inaccurate, particularly about dates, times and the exact sequence of events. Interview and questionnaire design requires considerable skill, as does interviewing itself, if it is to reflect the respondent's views rather than those of the researcher.

OBSERVATION

The observer attends the event and records what occurs there. The observer may be an outsider; for ▶ 8.4 example, a person watching court proceedings from the public gallery. Alternatively, the observer may be a person actually taking part in the events being described; for example, a police officer researching into the police force. Observation needs to be done systematically and accurately in order to avoid bias. Observers cannot record everything that they see. They must be careful that they do not record only what they want to see and neglect that which is unexpected and, perhaps, thereby unwelcome. One great difficulty in noting observations lies in deciding what to note down and what to omit. What seems unimportant at the time the notes were taken may take on a greater significance when a later analysis is made. It is important that the observer's record is contemporaneous, otherwise the data is weakened by what has been forgotten.

CHOOSING RESEARCH METHODS

For any particular piece of research, one method may be more suitable than another, because of ▶ 8.5 the nature of the data sources or the approach that the researcher wishes to take. If, for example, you want to research into the reasons litigants have for taking a case to court, there is little point in reading statements of claim because these may have been prepared by lawyers and are likely to reflect the legal requirements rather than the motivation for seeking redress via the courts. Here, the best place to start would be to interview (or send a questionnaire to) litigants. No single method can be said to provide the truth about every situation; some would argue that no method can provide the truth about any situation, for no one truth exists. Each method provides information based on the perceptions of the people who provide it, the record keepers, the interviewers or the observers.

Choice of research method depends not only on what information is sought but also on practicalities. The researcher may not be given access to records or permitted to carry out interviews. Professional bodies and employers are not always willing to let their members of staff participate in research. This may be because they consider the research unethical (perhaps requiring them to divulge information given in confidence), because they are too busy, because they do not see the value of the research or because they wish to conceal the very information in which the researcher is interested.

For many research studies more than one method is used to obtain a complete picture. However, practical matters, including budget and time limits, may mean that not every avenue of enquiry is pursued. What is important is that the methods chosen are appropriate to the subject of study, the approach of the researcher and the conclusions drawn.

SAMPLING

8.6 ▶ Looking at every case is not normally practical in research. Instead, the researcher takes a sample of cases. Thus, one may interview some lawyers or some defendants or observe, or read records at some courts. If a completely random sample is taken, then it should have the characteristics of the population as a whole. A sample of judges should, for example, include judges of the different ages, backgrounds and experience to be found amongst the judiciary. However, if a characteristic is very rare a sample may not contain any example of having that characteristic. The size of the sample and method of sampling must be chosen to fit with the study. In a study of attitudes of clients to lawyers there is clearly no point in interviewing only successful clients. The number of people refusing to take part in a study is also important. Researchers will try to obtain a high response rate (over 75 per cent) and also attempt to find out if those who refuse are likely to be different in any material way from those who agree to participate in the study.

RESEARCH FINDINGS

8.7 ▶ The account of any research will usually include some background information about the subject, the purpose of the study (the questions to be answered) and the methods used. Findings presented in words should cause no difficulty to the reader, but numbers may be quite confusing. Where comparisons are made, it is usually thought better to use *proportions* or *percentages* rather than actual numbers unless the numbers are very small. It is then important to be clear what the percentage represents: for example, was it 20 per cent of all plaintiffs or 20 per cent of successful plaintiffs. Some researchers do not give the actual figures, but prefer to use words such as "some", "most" or "the majority". This is not very helpful, since a word like "majority" can mean anything from 51 per cent to 99 per cent. If the numbers in a study are very small the use of percentages or proportions can itself be misleading. If a researcher looks at 10 people in their study and says 50 per cent of their sample said X this might look more impressive than saying 5 people said X.

There is a variety of ways of presenting figures so as to make them clearer. Tables (lists of figures) are commonly used because they make it easier to compare two or more categories or questions. Graphic presentation, using bar charts (histograms), pie charts or graphs, can create a clear overall impression of a complex set of figures.

Figure 1 below is a bar chart. It shows clearly the different numbers of offenders starting different types of probation orders for knife possession each quarter from 2008. Two main types of order were used, and the use of each declined over the period 2008–2012. This chart tells us nothing about the use of imprisonment for knife possession.

Figure 2 is a pie chart. The whole circle represents 100 per cent of the particular group. The segments represent different percentages. In this example, the exact percentages represented in the different segments have been printed on to the chart. This is not always done. Different circles represent the sentences of those with and without previous convictions for knife possession.

Figure 3 is a graph. This is probably the best way of showing a trend over time. The graph is designed to show the number of people in prison for knife possession between 2007 and 2012. The middle portion of the graph (2009–2010) contains no data. An explanation states that "due to technical problems relating to the supply of statistical data, it is not possible to provide figures" for this period.

As well as graphs and tables, most researchers will state the conclusions that they have drawn from the material and summarise the main findings of the study. It is crucial that the data should establish no more and no less than is stated in the conclusions. Some researchers make

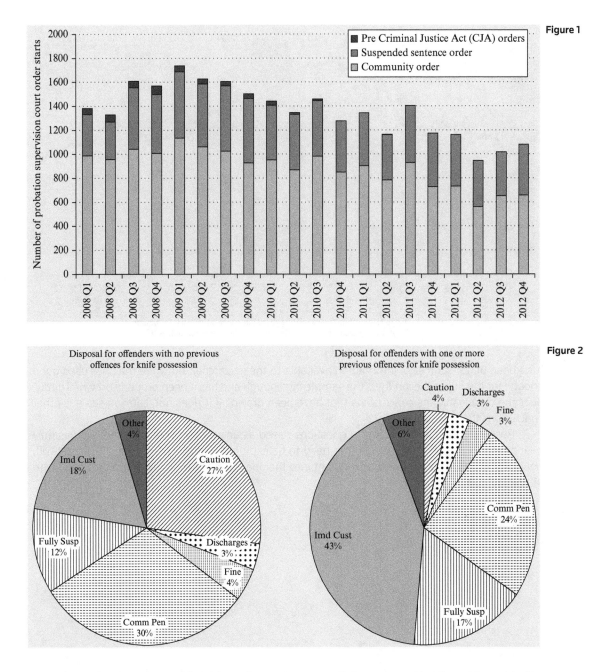

Figure 1

Disposal for offenders with no previous offences for knife possession

Disposal for offenders with one or more previous offences for knife possession

Figure 2

great claims for their data, whilst others do not draw out all the answers that it could provide. To avoid being persuaded by poor reasoning, look at the data and see what conclusions seem appropriate, then read the explanation given, and compare it with what you originally thought. A critical approach to any empirical research should always consider the following three questions. First, are the methods chosen appropriate? This includes both, "have the right questions been asked" and "have the right people (people who should know about the topic) been asked". There many

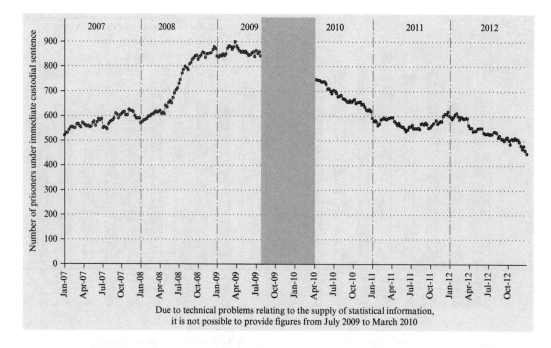

Due to technical problems relating to the supply of statistical information,
it is not possible to provide figures from July 2009 to March 2010

have been better sources of information available to the researcher, but were the ones used good enough for this study? Secondly, is the sample big enough and has it been properly drawn? Thirdly, does the data justify the conclusions that have been drawn? If it does not, can you see any other conclusions that it would justify?

Research often leaves as many questions raised as answers provided. Further studies may be indicated, interesting new areas that need to be explored. Studying this type of material will, hopefully, increase your interest and insight into the operation of law. It will not provide you with all the answers.

Figure 3

Exercise 5

READING RESEARCH MATERIALS

Reading and understanding research materials does not just involve seeing what conclusion the author has reached. Understanding the evidence the author or authors has for the conclusion drawn is as important as understanding the conclusion itself. This section is intended to improve your critical awareness of the materials that you are reading. Reading something critically means reading it to see what weaknesses there are in it. The fewer the weaknesses the stronger the conclusion will be. When reading something, remember that there are flaws in all articles and books. No author thinks their work is perfect. As a reader your task is to assess the merit of a particular argument by being aware of its weaknesses as well as its strengths. With practice critical reading will become an unconscious habit that you will bring to all your reading. Start by reading *Professional Minimalism? The Ethical Consciousness of Commercial Lawyers by Richard Moorhead and Victoria Hinchley*, the article reprinted below. When you have read the article once go back and read it again making detailed notes. When doing this, concentrate on trying to identify the arguments Smith et al. are trying to develop, paying close attention to the evidence that they present for the various points that they make. Your notes should tell you what the authors have written, the evidence they have based this on and what you think the limitations of their evidence are. When you think you understand the article, and have made your notes, try to answer the questions set out in Section A below. Refer to the original article when your notes give you insufficient information to answer the question. After you have finished the questions in Section A compare your answers with those that we have given at the back of this book. If your answers differ from ours you may need to go back and reread the article in order to get a better understanding of it. Once you are sure you understand the answers to Section A go on and complete the questions in Section B.

8.8

JOURNAL OF LAW AND SOCIETY
VOLUME 42, NUMBER 3, SEPTEMBER 2015
ISSN: 0263-323X, pp. 387–412

Professional Minimalism? The Ethical Consciousness of Commercial Lawyers

RICHARD MOORHEAD* AND VICTORIA HINCHLY**

This article investigates empirically, through semi-structured inter-views, what shapes the professional ethical consciousness of commercial lawyers. It considers in-house and private practice lawyers side by side, interrogating the view that in-house ethics are different and inferior to private practice to suggest as much similarity as difference. In both constituencies, and in very similar ways, professional ethical concepts are challenged by the pragmatic logics of business. We examine how their ethical logics are shaped by these pragmatic logics, suggesting how both groups of practitioners could sometimes be vulnerable to breaching the boundary between tenable zeal for the client and unethical or unlawful conduct. Although they conceive of themselves as ethical, the extent to which practitioners are well equipped, inclined and positively encouraged to work ethically within their own rules is open to question. As a result, we argue professional ethics exert minimal, superficial influence over a more self-interested, commercially-driven pragmatism.

INTRODUCTION

'Where were the lawyers?' is a familiar refrain in the United States after corporate scandals but less so in the United Kingdom. Recent events suggest that may be changing. Private practitioners and in-house lawyers have had a role in serious wrongdoing in banking and press hacking.[1] Allen & Overy

* UCL Faculty of Laws, Bentham House, Endsleigh Gardens, London WC1H
0EG, England
r.moorhead@ucl.ac.uk
** Department of Political Science, 1284 University of Oregon, Eugene, OR
97403-1284, United States of America
vhinchly@uoregon.edu

1 D. Kershaw and R. Moorhead, 'Consequential Responsibility for Client Wrongs: Lehman Brothers and the Regulation of the Legal Profession' (2013) 76 *Modern Law*

has been accused of putting inappropriate pressure on a prosecution witness.[2] Clifford Chance litigated a client's fraud case which was found to be artificial and 'replete with defects, illogicalities and inherent improbabilities',[3] raising serious professional misconduct issues.[4] Evidence during a Russian Oligarch's trials was 'polished'.[5] Two former Barclays General Counsel (GCs) have been interviewed under caution.[6] Internationally, in-house lawyers in General Motors and private practitioners advising BNP Paribas have been in the spotlight.[7]

A variety of explanations might be given for such cases. Chief amongst these is the concern that the practice of law as a profession is increasingly being replaced with the practice of law as a business. Under such a view, the growing power and status of in-house lawyers marks the increasing power of big business over the lawyers it employs and instructs, whilst private practices emulate the business structures and attitudes of their clients, competing more fiercely with each other for the work.[8] The influence of business on law is not a new phenomenon,[9] but the rise of global practices and large, powerful in-house legal teams almost certainly represents an escalation of commercial and business logics within practice. In turn, professional bodies have questioned the adequacy of education and training in the field of ethics.[10] The

Rev. 26; R. Moorhead, 'On the Wire' *New Law J.*, 17 August 2012, 1080; a prosecution of an in-house and a private practice lawyer is pending before the Solicitors' Disciplinary Tribunal, at <http://www.sra.org.uk/sra/news/press/statement-chapman-abramson-sdt-august-2014.page>.

2 C. Binham and J. Croft, 'Allen and Overy put pressure on prosecution witness, court hears' *Financial Times*, 6 November 2013.

3 *Excalibur Ventures LLC* v. *Texas Keystone Inc and others* [2013] EWHC 4278 (Comm).

4 R. Moorhead, 'Excalibur raises serious professional conduct concerns for Clifford Chance' (2014), at <http://lawyerwatch.wordpress.com/2014/01/15/excalibur-raises-serious-professional-conduct-concerns-for-clifford-chance/>.

5 *Berezovsky* v. *Abramovich* [2012] EWHC B15 (Ch).

6 C. Binham, 'Ex Barclays bankers to give evidence to fraud agency' *Financial Times*, 24 September 2014, at <http://www.ft.com/cms/s/0/950db234-4406-11e4-8abd-00144feabdc0.html#axzz3S1JCqMOS>.

7 M.B. Neitz, 'Shades of Enron: the Legal Ethics Implications of the General Motors Scandal', at <http://www.legalethicsforum.com/blog/2014/06/professor-michele-benedetto-neitz-shades-of-enron-the-legal-ethics-implications-of-the-general-motor.html>; *U.S.* v. *BNP Paribas SA*, U.S. District Court, Southern District of New York, No. 14-cr-00460, Statement of Facts, at <http://www.justice.gov/sites/default/files/opa/legacy/2014/06/30/statement-of-facts.pdf>.

8 L.E. Ribstein, 'The Death of Big Law' (2010) *Wisconsin Law Rev.* 749; J. Faulconbridge and D. Muzio, 'Organizational Professionalism in Globalizing Law Firms' (2008) 22 *Work, Employment & Society* 7; D. Muzio, D.M. Brock, and R. Suddaby, 'Professions and Institutional Change: Towards an Institutionalist Sociology of the Professions' (2013) 50 *J. of Management Studies* 699.

9 See, for example, D.L. Rhode, 'Ethical Perspectives on Legal Practice' (1985) 37 *Stanford Law Rev.* 589.

10 A. Boon, *Legal Ethics at the Initial Stage?: A Model Curriculum* (2010); K. Economides and J. Rogers, *Preparatory Ethics Training for Future Solicitors* (2009).

Legal Education and Training Review (LETR) commissioned by the three lead professional regulators evidenced a strong professional consensus about the need for education in the area.[11]

Given the general concern about in-house lawyering and the very visible influence of business logics on private practice, it is perhaps surprising that there has been almost no empirical study of the professional ethics of commercial lawyers in England and Wales.[12] This is doubly surprising given the importance of London as a centre for global business. Even in the United States, where there is a larger body of work, the literature concentrates on in-house lawyers. Work directly comparing in-house and private practitioners is largely absent.

This article begins to redress that imbalance. We focus on senior solicitors in large solicitors' firms and in-house lawyers in blue-chip corporate and public sector roles. Drawing on semi-structured interviews with twenty-one commercial lawyers, we sought to understand how our respondents understood ethics to be relevant to their role. Whilst we were interested in how they understood ethics in the broadest sense, our principal focus was on how they understood their professional obligations under the law and their code of conduct. As such, we sought to understand how they saw their role as professionals and their approach to professional principles and rules. Were the commercial and pragmatic logics of professional businesses and business clients emphasized in the work of sociologists and management scientists tempered by a clearly articulated consciousness of professional obligations? We are also able to directly compare the differences between in-house and private practice lawyers.

Our analysis suggests that the professional ethical consciousness of commercial lawyers in-house or in private practice is minimalistic in a number of ways. We are not suggesting this leads to routine unethicality. A minimalistic approach is consistent – up to a point – with the standard, if regularly criticized, conception of zealous lawyering.[13] Minimalism does,

---

11 Legal Education and Training Review (LETR), *Setting Standards: The future of legal services education and training regulation in England and Wales* (2013) Executive Summary.

12 Flood has written thoughtfully about ethics amongst global lawyers, see, for example, J. Flood, 'Transnational Lawyering: Clients, Ethics and Regulation' in *Lawyers in Practice: Ethical Decision Making in Context*, eds. L. Mather and L.C. Levin (2012), but his empirical work focuses on commercial lawyers from a sociological rather ethical perspective. Griffiths-Baker's study of conflict of interests had a significant focus on commercial firms, see J. Griffiths-Baker, *Serving Two Masters: Conflicts of Interest in the Modern Law Firm* (2002).

13 S.L Pepper, 'The Lawyer's Amoral Ethical Role: A Defense, a Problem, and Some Possibilities' (1986) *Am. Bar Foundation Research J.* 24; D. Markovits, *A Modern Legal Ethics: Adversary Advocacy in a Democratic Age* (2009); C. Fried, 'Lawyer as Friend: The Moral Foundations of the Lawyer-Client Relation' (1975) 85 *Yale Law J.* 1060; T. Dare, 'Mere-Zeal, Hyper-Zeal and the Ethical Obligations of Lawyers' (2004) 7 *Legal Ethics* 24–38.

however, suggest vulnerabilities where the boundary between tenable zeal for the client and unethical or unlawful conduct can be breached. The extent to which practitioners are well-equipped, inclined, and positively encouraged to work ethically within their own rules is open to question.

EXISTING WORK ON THE ETHICS OF COMMERCIAL LAWYERS

Much work on commercial lawyers concentrates on in-house lawyers. It tends to explore the ways in which the in-house role may be more ethically problematic than a private practice counterpart. Jenoff, the most forceful, argues that in-housers are embedded within business and rendered unable to advise independently; they are incentivized to comply with executive diktats and socialized to identify with corporate objectives.[14] For her, heavy involvement in decision-making removes their objectivity.[15]

In contrast, in-house lawyers might be employed for their relative independence from the business:[16] 'if professionals are not able to retain sufficient independence ... [why] pay a premium for their skills?'[17] This argument suggests a choice: the skills and apparent professionalism of a lawyer can be usefully deployed towards evasion, avoidance or creative compliance with the law[18] or they can be deployed towards independent interpretation and application of the law. Which role is chosen for or by in-house lawyers? Nelson and Nielsen define three archetypes: cops, willing to say no when corporate wrongdoing is contemplated; counsellors, who might counsel against unlawful or unethical action, but leave decisions to the business; and, entrepreneurs who might exploit law aggressively as a source of commercial advantage.[19] In their study, cops were a minority and counsellors the most common.[20] In contrast, Rostain's more recent pilot work has emphasized a belief that corporate governance reforms had strengthened the hand of GCs in resisting wrongdoing.[21]

---

14 P. Jenoff, 'Going Native: Incentive, Identity, and the Inherent Ethical Problem of In-House Counsel' (2011) 114 *West Virginia Law Rev.* 725.

15 id.

16 H.P. Gunz and S.P. Gunz, 'The Lawyer's Response to Organizational Professional Conflict: An Empirical Study of the Ethical Decision Making of in-House Counsel' (2002) 39 *Am. Business Law J.* 248.

17 id.

18 D. McBarnet and C. Whelan, 'The Elusive Spirit of the Law: Formalism and the Struggle for Legal Control' (1991) 54 *Modern Law Rev.* 848.

19 R.L. Nelson and L.B. Nielsen, 'Cops, Counsel, and Entrepreneurs: Constructing the Role of inside Counsel in Large Corporations' (2000) 34 *Law & Society Rev.* 457.

20 id., pp. 468–9.

21 T. Rostain, 'General Counsel in the Age of Compliance: Preliminary Findings and New Research Questions' (2008) 21 *Georgetown J. of Legal Ethics*, 465, at 474.

An assumption tending to underlie these studies is that in-house ethics are different *and inferior* to private practice. The assumption drives questions about the ethicality of in-house lawyers that inform European Court of Justice (ECJ) decisions on legal professional privilege.[22] Assumptions about the relative virtues of private practitioners inform their appointment as independent investigators and corporate monitors[23] as well as otherwise acting as reputational intermediaries between clients and regulators.[24] They are supported by a limited number of American studies supporting the ethicality of large law firms.[25] A series of professional scandals has eroded belief in the ethicality of elite law[26] but the assumption that, in the commercial field, in-house lawyers are the most prone to ethical problems tends to remain.

There are some thoughtful dissents. Seeing in-house lawyers as subject to a binary divide between being client-captured or independent may be too reductive.[27] Langevoort explores the risks posed by in-housers 'getting too comfortable' with client preferences, but suggests the pressures may not now be so different in private practice.[28] His suggestion – albeit one not evidenced – is that commercial and cognitive incentives on private practitioners to do the client's bidding are great, as is the case for in-house lawyers. Kim suggests that the place of in-house lawyers in the corporate network may mean they are better placed than outside practitioners to exert influence, if not control, over corporate wrongdoing.[29] They have more information and more opportunities to influence conduct and so may have a stronger ethical role than outside lawyers. She also takes the most nuanced position on independence: in-house lawyers may shift between cop, counsellor, and entrepreneurial roles to match their behaviour to the nature of the risk in questions and the reporting obligations that are placed upon them.[30]

22 *Akzo Nobel Chemicals Ltd and Akcros Chemicals Ltd* v. *European Commission.* Case C-550/07 P, Reports of Cases 2010 I-08301 (Court of Justice, Grand Chamber 2010).
23 There are numerous examples: Lord Gold was appointed as independent monitor at BAE. Law firms are often appointed to investigate or assist in investigating existing clients, for example, Reed Smith were appointed to advise the BBC's investigation into why its *Newsnight* programme dropped a Jimmy Saville documentary.
24 J.C. Coffee Jr., 'The Attorney as Gatekeeper: An Agenda for the SEC' (2003) 103 *Columbia Law Rev.* 1293.
25 In particular, E.O. Smigel, *The Wall Street Lawyer, Professional Organization Man?* (1969) and S.P. Shapiro, *Tangled Loyalties: Conflict of Interest in Legal Practice* (2002).
26 Most recently in the field of tax: see T. Rostain and M.C. Regan Jr., *Confidence Games: Lawyers, Accountants, and the Tax Shelter Industry* (2014); J.M. Conley and S. Baker, 'Fall from Grace or Business as Usual? A Retrospective Look at Lawyers on Wall Street and Main Street' (2005) 30 *Law & Social Inquiry* 783.
27 R. Dinovitzer, H. Gunz, and S. Gunz, 'Unpacking Client Capture: Evidence from Corporate Law Firms' (2014) 2 *J. of Professions and Organization* 99.
28 D.C. Langevoort, 'Getting (Too) Comfortable: In-House Lawyers, Enterprise Risk, and the Financial Crisis' (2012) *Wisconsin Law Rev.* 495
29 S.H. Kim, 'Gatekeepers Inside Out' (2008) 21 *Georgetown J. of Legal Ethics* 411.
30 S.H. Kim, 'The Ethics of In-House Practice' in Mather and Levin (eds.), op. cit., n. 12.

Importantly, Kim's point suggests a closer need to tie essentially sociological understandings of role back to specific legal and professional obligations.

Positions on the relative ethicality of in-house and private practice are not generally supported by empirical study which compares the two groups together. Indeed, there has been little empirical research on the ethicality of commercial lawyers in private practice. Kirkland's recent study is of interest. She finds ethics in law firms determined by pragmatic or bureaucratic norms rather than being firmly linked to external standards of right or professional conduct.[31] What matters is the 'norms one's superiors would follow, principles can only be guidelines, ethics can only be etiquette, and values can only be tastes.'[32] Power relationships render partners dependent on clients and associates dependent on partners and this renders 'notions of right and wrong, proper and improper, mutable in the lawyers' eyes.'[33] Other work emphasizes that lawyers are influenced by their clients and their firms but they also have some agency; they have opportunities for resistance or influence.[34] Conversely, a neo-institutional perspective suggests that 'Professional identities [now form] ... around logics of efficiency and commerce which have displaced traditional logics of ethics and public service.'[35]

In this study we are able to compare how in-house and private practitioner lawyers (say they) think about ethics, and can thus engage in a more direct comparison of the two groups within one study. We are also able to add a perspective from England and Wales to the literature on in-house and commercial lawyers. More specifically still, the study takes forward the need for attention to specific professional ethics obligations when considering debates about commercial lawyers. Our focus in this article is primarily on the lawyer's obligation to 'uphold the rule of law and the proper administration of justice'.[36] Finally, the claims of interactionists and neo-institutional approaches raise an important question: given institutional and commercial influences on professional identity and behaviour, do professional ethics exert influence over a more self-interested, commercially-driven pragmatism?

31 K. Kirkland, 'Ethics in Large Law Firms: The Principle of Pragmatism' (2005) 35 *University of Memphis Law Rev.* 631. See, also, R.L. Nelson, *Partners with Power: The Social Transformation of the Large Law Firm* (1988) and the report, 'Ethics: Beyond the Rules' (1998) 67 *Fordham Law Rev.* 691.
32 id., p. 639.
33 id., p. 712.
34 T. Kuhn, 'Positioning Lawyers: Discursive Resources, Professional Ethics and Identification' (2009) 16 *Organization* 681–704.
35 Muzio et al., op. cit., n. 8, p. 700.
36 Solicitors Regulation Authority (SRA), *SRA Handbook and Code of Conduct* (2011) Principle 1.

METHODOLOGY

Understanding professional ethics is complex. Ethical questions being foundationally controversial and real problems rarely being public, they are difficult to capture empirically as 'fact'. A full suite of empirical approaches would tend to involve understanding:[37]

- Character (disposition, personal values, attitudes, role morality);
- Context (economic and social incentives, infrastructure and culture including the decision rules employed); and,
- Capacity (aptitude to recognize issues, knowledge of the rules, reasoning processes demonstrated through ability to weigh competing interests, skills in persuasion of colleagues and others towards ethical ends.)

Each dimension may interrelate: character may influence how we see context, context may influence our capacities, and so on. The importance of context in influencing ethical behaviour is well established.[38] Ethical reasoning skills are measurable and important.[39] Yet, moral and behavioural psychology opens up new research agendas relevant to understanding lawyers' ethics.[40] Some suggest ethics is more intuitive than rational[41] and prone to identifiable biases.[42]

Accordingly, we see ethical consciousness as a site for studying the competing dimensions of ethicality: character, context, and capacity; the intuitive and rational; structures and agency. Just as legal consciousness has been employed to recast our study of rules,[43] and the experience of law,[44] 'habitual patterns of talk and action' about ethics may help illuminate practitioners' 'common-sense understanding of the world'.[45]

We also use consciousness as a self-aware or self-limiting term, to conjure up the ephemerality of the concept and the elusive relationship between conscious, subconscious, and intuitive thinking. In studying how lawyers think about ethics, we recognize significant limits on our ability to identify thought. Ultimately we cannot prove what is going on in someone else's

---

37 R. Moorhead et al., *Designing Ethics Indicators for Legal Services Provision* (2012).
38 See, for example, Mather and Levin (eds.), op. cit., n. 12.
39 For example, J. Rest et al., 'Alchemy and Beyond: Indexing the Defining Issues Test' (1997) *J. of Educational Psychology* 498.
40 A.M. Perlman, 'A Behavioral Theory of Legal Ethics' (2013), at <http://papers.ssrn.com/abstract=2320605>.
41 J. Haidt, *The Righteous Mind: Why Good People Are Divided by Politics and Religion* (2013); F. Cushman et al., 'Multi-System Moral Psychology' in *The Moral Psychology Handbook*, eds. J.M. Doris et al. (2010) 47.
42 For example, Langevoort, op. cit., n. 28.
43 A. Sarat, 'Law Is All Over: Power, Resistance and the Legal Consciousness of the Welfare Poor' (1990) 2 *Yale J. of Law & the Humanities* 343, at 345.
44 P. Ewick and S.S. Silbey, *The Common Place of Law: Stories from Everyday Life* (1998) 3.
45 S. Merry, *Getting Justice and Getting Even: Legal Consciousness among Working-Class Americans* (1990).

head. Indeed, we do not always know for ourselves what is driven by intuitions rather than conscious thought or what we wish to hide.[46] Yet there is significant value in exploring someone's experience of their own mind.[47]

In this study, twenty-one interviews were conducted with interviewees recruited from elite practice: twelve were employed in large companies (FTSE 100) and public sector organizations and nine in the kinds of private-practice firms typically instructed by the in-house lawyers within our sample (very large firms, often with an international practice). Of the twelve in-house lawyers, ten were solicitors, one had qualified as a barrister, and another had qualified as a barrister and a solicitor. They were also generally senior practitioners, often General Counsel or equivalent, though some were heads of smaller sub-divisions (such as compliance and litigation). The majority had upwards of twenty years' experience. All the private practitioners were solicitors and were generally a senior group (seven partners had been qualified in excess of thirty years).

Although we attempted to engage both senior and junior lawyers to allow for likely divergence in perceptions,[48] junior lawyers were markedly less likely to agree to talk to us. Even the most junior lawyers in the in-house sample had upwards of ten years' experience. Two of the private practitioners had less than ten years' experience. Four of our interviewees were women: three of those worked in-house.

As with all qualitative work, we emphasize that we should not necessarily regard our interviewee views as typical. This is not a sample designed to be representative of all commercial lawyers but one which explores the views of a select and very senior group of elite lawyers. Interviewees often said in agreeing to speak to us that they felt that they had 'got their house in order' ethically or otherwise; they signalled their elite status (say as 'sector leaders') and comfort with their organization's approach to ethics. Interestingly, some identified themselves as having been aggressive risk takers in the past. Some of our participants' organizations were also affected by significant scandals during or after the course of the research, suggesting that the past returned to haunt them or the ethical present was less sturdy than they thought.

Semi-structured interviews were conducted over the telephone. To reduce defensiveness and mitigate the temptation to give answers which reflected a social desirability bias, participants were told that we were not testing their

---

46 J. Craigie, 'Thinking and feeling: moral deliberation in a dual-process framework' (2011) 24 *Philosophical Psychology* 53; J. Graham et al., 'Mapping the Moral Domain' (2011) 101 *J. of Personality and Social Psychology* 366.

47 D. Dennett, 'Quining qualia' in *Consciousness in Contemporary Science*, eds. A. Marcel and E. Bisiach (1992).

48 L.K.Trevio et al., 'It's lovely at the top: Hierarchical levels, identities and perceptions of organizational ethics' (2008) 18 *Business Ethics Q.* 233; C. Parker and L. Aitken, 'The Queensland "Workplace Culture Check": Learning from Reflection on Ethics Inside Law Firms' (2011) 24 *Georgetown J. of Legal Ethics* 399.

ethicality, although we were exploring their ethical reasoning. The usual protections of anonymity were given. It was also emphasized that the research was exploratory, independent, and not sponsored by a regulator (which some wanted reassurance on).

Interview schedules provided a series of questions to act as a semi-structured conversation between interviewer and interviewee based on our reading of the relevant literature.[49] The questions explored views on what ethics meant to them; what they thought were the most important values or principles governing how a lawyer should behave; the influence of business incentives on ethics; and how ethics were assured within their organizations.[50] Interviews are, at best, verbal articulations of consciousness rather than consciousness itself.[51] Accurate reporting requires honest, articulate, diligent and self-aware communication. Error, omission, and memory lapse are potential problems, as are response biases designed to show the interviewee in a good light.[52] One way of mitigating these risks is by asking the participant to report on an experience in the immediate moment, rather than whilst recalling previous conduct. For this reason our research approach employed vignettes as part of the interview process: problems which each interviewee was asked to give their response to. These are ethical problems which respondents are asked to 'solve' there and then. The risks are only mitigated by such an approach; they are not removed.

ANALYSIS

In the next sections of the article we discuss our analysis of the interviews. Interviews were coded thematically, with the interview topic guides forming the basis of the coding framework. NVivo was used to assist in organizing and coding the data. Here we draw out the most important themes emerging from the interviews.

1. *Ethics as not being criminal*

Respondents were first asked what came to mind as ethics in legal practice. This tended to prompt responses suggesting a mixture of honesty, integrity, and serving the client. Some in-house lawyers mentioned their Company's Code of Conduct. Bribery came up regularly, being topical because of the introduction of the Bribery Act 2010. Several in-house lawyers, in emphasizing their duty to do the best for their client, raised tensions between

---

49 See, in particular, Moorhead et al., op. cit, n. 37.
50 The schedules are available on request, see address on p. 387.
51 B. Baars, *A Cognitive Theory of Consciousness* (1993) 15–18.
52 See, for example, D.M. Randall and M.F. Fernandes, 'The Social Desirability Response Bias in Ethics Research' (1991) 10 *J. of Business Ethics* 805.

commercial aims, law, and the lawyer's role as an employee. In this way, a concern about independence became apparent.

To return to Nelson and Neilson's archetypes, our sample of in-house lawyers generally saw themselves as counsellors or technicians and not as cops. As counsellors, they advised, but they did not take responsibility. The notion of a grey zone suggested something legally or ethically problematic about a course of action that flowed from (or was assisted by) advice. Our lawyers generally had no difficulty distancing themselves from ethical responsibility for these grey zones, commonly falling back on the mantra of: 'I advise, but the client decides.' Here a lawyer takes the position one step further: they facilitate understanding but the client (the business) interprets the grey zones. IH11 said:

> [I] always make sure that the client ... understand[s] the law. I think they also need to understand what the law is trying to achieve, so that if there is a grey area they know the correct way to interpret it.

These grey zones plainly gave rise to a tension in the lawyers' minds. Although they professed comfort with greyness, many discussed a tension with legality. How did this tension manifest itself? There was widespread acceptance that a narrow, legalistic 'what can I get away with' interpretation of law might damage the client's interests. Doing the 'right' thing rather than simply the legally permitted thing was sometimes seen as commercially wise and ethical. Equally, most suggested limits to their ability to say no to a client, even where they might consider this a legitimate part of their role. They were constrained by a number of factors.

First, the only notion of unlawfulness which appeared to restrain respondents consistently was *criminality*. Respondents regularly distinguished tolerable legal risk from potentially criminal activity, acting, 'not [in] a criminal way, but act in a way which is in the best interests of the client rather than always necessarily following your advice ...' (IH11). Even where an in-houser emphasized 'being the conscience of the organization ... not only sticking to the law but also the letter of the law', the interviewee had experienced being asked to 'find a way around something which is an absolute prohibition' (IH12). Another said that law only restrains if 'there isn't a way around it' (IH2).

A second way of looking at the problem was seeing the lawyer's job as ensuring an informed cost-benefit calculation when behaving in a potentially unlawful way, or generating sufficiently plausible claims to legality to minimize the risk of regulatory action or third-party litigation. The calculation was not 'is something lawful?' but whether the commercial benefits of action outweigh the risks of regulatory infraction or civil suit. Whilst some respondents thought they might exert ethical influence as part of the process of weighing costs and benefits, the technical competence of the lawyer was ultimately employed in examining the limits of the law, not the ethicality of the decision.

Not all respondents were comfortable with this. Tensions were evident across a range of respondents: IH6 talked of risks to independence in the 'general conflicts in terms of the [in-house] role'; IH4 about 'ill-advised activity by some senior managers, which have [sic] cropped up occasionally'; and IH10 'the demands of management to do certain things, which may not always be either legal or may kind of hover on the edge of illegality.'

Seeing unlawfulness as risk operated to both recognize and normalize the tension between whether a course of action was lawful or unlawful. In framing a decision as risk-based, ambiguity and potential unlawfulness was tolerated. They were the facilitator of calculated risk taking with law. Where legal risk is unavoidable, and risks are neutrally weighed, this may be unexceptional. Yet, in balancing risk, the lawyers acted as guardians of their client interests not as independent administrators of the rule of law. They recognized that the boundaries of tolerable risk were malleable and open to interpretation and that corporate dynamics (generally) pushed in one direction: don't say no, say how. There was a strong sense of the reputational cost to a lawyer in saying '"No, you can't do certain things", or "I'm sorry but certain things are required" ... they don't like it' (IH10).

Private practitioners recognized similar gradations of tolerable unlawfulness. Some suggested even narrower tests: 'knowing participation in criminality' (PP1) or 'straight dishonesty' (PP7). 'Non-criminal' regulation had significantly less resonance. When making these kinds of comments, in-house and private practice interviewees were often distinguishing 'regulation' from more criminal prohibition in a somewhat hazy way.[53]

They too were informed by an incorrect but strongly held assumption that clients' interests were pre-eminent. A regulatory framework, or the law in general, might establish a broad idea of what was probably expected or required, but if there was ambiguity and the client had a weak (but runnable) argument, then that too was permitted. PP1, for example, was willing to assist with actions which were, in his judgement, arguably, but probably not, lawful. They can advance, in his view, the 'wrong' argument. He contrasted criminal liability: '... Certainly, we'd never get involved' (PP1). The aim was not to establish legality but defensibility:

> ... it's not for us necessarily to consider the wider public interest.... we don't need to necessarily think in the same way the regulator might about wider issues and wider implications. We just need to make sure that our clients stay within the law and if they do that, their position will be defensible. (PP6)

---

53 Whilst practitioners distinguished regulatory requirements, 'criminal' prohibitions, and civil obligations, the distinctions are not conceptually clear-cut: see, for example, M. Dyson, *Unravelling Tort and Crime* (2014).

The impact of this was that 'within the law' means it is *arguably* legal not that it is *clearly or probably* legal, and arguability may provide a generously low threshold. The law of negligence may, in some ways, drive lawyers towards such an approach by allowing loss of chance claims to be advanced where the prospects of success may be low.[54] To avoid being negligent in litigation, the need to advance all plausible claims may thus drive towards saying the client can bring claims (or – by analogy for transactional lawyers – take steps) where the prospects of success (by analogy – legality) is questionable.

2. *Wariness of the public interest*

The narrow view that the client should be promoted first with only the criminal law providing significant restraint is the ethics of zealous advocacy, though even the strongest academic versions of zeal emphasize that lawyers should be restrained by the law and their rules of conduct.[55] The Solicitors' Code of Conduct requires a principle-based approach to professional ethics. This requires solicitors to uphold the rule of law and the proper administration of justice; act with independence; and act in the best interests of each *client*.[56]

> Where two or more *Principles* come into conflict the one which takes precedence is the one which best serves the public interest in the particular circumstances, especially the public interest in the proper administration of justice.[57]

In simple terms, then, the rules specify that public interest concerns can trump client interest concerns where there is a conflict between the professional principles. One's own economic or other interests as a lawyer are subservient to both.

The 'grey zones' discussed above provide an interesting testing ground for the application of this principle. As we have seen, our respondents indicated, in general, that non-criminal activity, 'sort of on the edge of commercial practice' (IH11), would be tolerated. Pushes towards creative or selective compliance took place against a management who, 'want to know how far can they go before they breach the criminal law' (IH11). At what point is the obligation to law and the administration of justice engaged sufficiently to trump the client's interest? The Code of Conduct does not confine itself to behaviour which is criminal – and if it did one would have a legitimate question to ask about the idea of the profession: if the rule is simply do not act criminally then that is a rule which applies to all, not just

---

54 *Sharpe* v. *Addison* [2003] All E.R. (D) 403 (Jul).
55 See references at n. 13, above.
56 SRA, op. cit., n. 36, Part 1.
57 id.

professional lawyers. Equally, the law is tolerant of deliberate breaches of contract and the like where remedies can be found in damages. There is a balance to be struck, but how should it be struck?

We asked respondents to focus more explicitly on this question by rating in order of importance the public interest, the client's interest, and the firm's (or their own) commercial interest. Generally, for our interviewees, client interests came unequivocally first. This was particularly true of private practitioners though even here there were some expressions of anxiety around instructions that had been accepted from banks. For example:

> I myself have always wanted to avoid situations where we just take on work because the institutions want us to do it, even though I think to some extent, we shouldn't be doing it ...
> (PP3)

Generally, there was a wariness of notions of the public interest which respondents saw as subjective and difficult to define:

> I don't think ... the law should rely on public interest. If the law hasn't caught up ... it's not my duty to do that. I will leave that to legislators and other people ...
> (IH12)

Some criticized the public interest ideas as populist, 'the old 20/20 hindsight problem' (PP5), or saw companies as purely economic creatures generally operating in a moral vacuum:

> companies aren't in a position to have morals, they haven't got a soul ... [They are] taking actually what are not moral or ethical decisions once you are outside the area where this is straight dishonesty ...
> (PP7)

Where law was imperfect, where ambiguity created space for doubt about right or wrong, that space was typically inhabited by the client (in the shape of those giving them instructions) not any obligation to promote the rule of law. An opposite view, that ambiguity creates a space where ethical judgements are possible, perhaps essential, was usually resisted by our respondents:

> ... you're not here to judge moral issues ... the client has retained you to advise ... it's not for you to judge the morality of it ...
> (IH4)

The risk inherent in a minimalist approach to restraining clients can be captured in the mutual convenience of divided responsibility. Lawyers advise that the law does not prohibit it and the clients say 'our lawyers said we could do it'. Ambiguity is helpfully defined as within the law. Such shifts in understanding may be deliberate or accidental conveniences. It was a problem at least some of our respondents were conscious of. PP1 suggested lawyers needed to keep their antennae up to prevent being taken advantage of by clients as vehicles for dishonesty. PP6 was similarly cognisant of the

399

role of the lawyer as reputational intermediary, where grey areas could be sanctified by the giving of legal advice:

> And if the law firm has given them advice that it's legal, then they can go to the regulator and ... say, 'we've taken legal advice and we're comfortable'. (PP6)

It is also worth emphasizing that scepticism of public interest was not universal. In-house lawyers were somewhat more likely than private practitioners to suggest the public interest came first. Some claimed that corporate codes and cultures of doing the right thing supported this. Judgement calls went beyond purely legal requirements because their company had a 'very strong sense of public purpose' (IH9) or because 'ethical and reputational [reasons]' (IH9) required it. Perhaps too they could not as easily rely on a distinction between them as the lawyer-adviser and the 'client' as morally autonomous, as they were part of the business:

> ultimately we have to do what we think is right regardless of what the company wants or what the ... stakeholders/clients want. (IH10)

Some respondents also described more interpersonal notions of ethics: for example, IH1's 'the way we conduct ourselves as a business' limiting opportunistic bargaining or PP2's 'openness with clients and how you deal with people' or PP8's 'being able to accept the word of another practitioner ... [and] conducting themselves in a proper and appropriate kind of way'. What was notably absent from much of the discussion was any notion of *professional* responsibility. Very few lawyers we spoke to utilized principles within their professional Code to protect their professional independence or to frame the judgements they took in the grey zones. Where they did so, they tended to refer only to their obligation not to mislead the court. Beyond adherence to notions of criminal legality, rule of law considerations had minimal purchase. For private practitioners, where anxiety about sharp practice by a client became acute and/or prolonged, this was accompanied by an approach to professional ethics which emphasized 'quiet exit' from the client relationship and not acting for very controversial clients, or 'acting [only] for the sorts of clients we would want to be associated with reputationally' (PP9).

3. *Contextual pressures*

Scholars have suggested that framing a problem in terms of commerciality leads to a general weakening of ethical sensitivity,[58] or that the need to establish and maintain relationships within the organization or with the client

---

58 See M. Kouchaki et al., 'Seeing Green: Mere Exposure to Money Triggers a Business Decision Frame and Unethical Outcomes' (2013) 12 *Organizational Behavior and Human Decision Processes* 153.

have similar effects.[59] When asked in general how they rated public, firm/ own, and client interests, most in-housers tended to say they placed their own interests a distant third place. Interestingly, though, private practitioners often put their firm's commercial interest *before* the public interest and sometimes pointed to situations where the firm's interests would come before the client's interests (principally in decisions about clients who might not fit reputationally). Some even suggested that, in fact, the firm's interests might be pre-eminent. If this view influences their practice, then this is the mirror image of what their Code of Conduct expects.

To delve into the issue of context more deeply, we asked about the influence of the business on their ethics. When asked whether billing, targets or other economic pressures impacted on their ethical decision making, most respondents suggested not. In-housers usually distanced themselves from the potential downsides of performance related bonuses:

> my bonus is based on the profitability of [the] company ... there's nothing ... [I could do] that would really move that needle one way or the other. [Also] ... it's sufficiently geared towards my performance ... my performance personally ... there's nothing ethical that would make a difference to that ...
> (IH1)

The answer is contradictory: a bonus geared toward personal performance means the needle can be moved. The interviewee's point is that ethicality was not assessed because ethical conduct was taken as a given not in tensions with other performance indicators. Others thought bonuses could *encourage* ethicality ('if we don't meet our targets for training or ... give examples of leadership in the ethical or compliance area ... that impacts on your bonus' (IH11)), but avoided saying they could do the reverse. Others simply emphasized their own independence as a bulwark against bonuses driving questionable behaviour.

Some concerns *were* expressed about what a general pressure to deliver on work too quickly could do:

> It's not about trying to be unlawful at all, or ... rejoicing in illegalities but managing the tensions between the rightful objectives of the organization and the requirements of the law.
> (IH10)

A general culture of getting things done, or thinking of the bottom line could cause problems, but we also heard of in-housers being deliberately managed towards 'thinking the unthinkable':

> [O]k, you're not really being asked to make it happen ... you're being asked to ... brainstorm these ideas which you feel deeply uncomfortable about ... how can we kind of slide this under someone's radar ... how can we get away with something ... we kind of know we shouldn't be doing, and that's the kind of

---

59 See references at nn. 16–33, above.

pressure you always get in organizations, there's always people who ... [are] not constrained by any particular professional code, you know ... they just want to ... do something to make the management happy.
(IH10)

Private practitioners were more inclined to see a potential problem with targets and bonuses but typically said these problems did not apply to them, or that sophisticated clients did not need protection (suggesting they did not perceive public interest risks inherent in commercial incentives). In private practice, lockstep and departmental, rather than individual billing, targets were also held up as inhibiting dangers. Overbilling was sometimes said to have occurred *in the past* yet every lawyer knew high billing could 'only improve their reputation and their chances ...' (PP3) or that hourly billing and targets presented, 'a temptation which in my view, you must always resist' (PP4). PP1 suggested targets were not taken overly seriously, and were simply part of 'any commercial organization', but also that for 'bonuses, the most important factor is contribution to fees'. Comfort was also taken from the idea that billing pressures are worse elsewhere (in the United States in particular). There is a whiff of relativist thinking here: we can't have a problem, because somewhere else is worse, whilst 'any commercial organization' is the same.

The idea that targets are not meant to incentivize behaviour begs the question, why are they there? PP6, a non-partner, acknowledged problems more directly and did not portray them as historic:

It's probably something probably pretty fundamental to the way law firms work ... the way law firms bill creates all kinds of issues for lawyers ... the reality is everybody will put down hours that make it look like they are doing the seven hours a day even if they are not ... there is such a link between performance and promotion and bonus payments that come off of that that people will always put down more hours, regardless of whether those hours are actually a hundred per cent accurate.... if you don't do your seven hours one day, you will get an email saying 'you haven't done your hours' and then questions will come in and if it goes on too long, then you will start getting a red light above your name with partners or senior partners, so the culture is, the whole way it's set up is very much set up to encourages associates to make sure associates put their seven hours down every day.

PP9 described targets as 'incredibly motivating' for 'some people'. They also pointed to an important narrowing of professional values which occurred if law firm management is too reductively numbers-oriented:

... more effort ... should be made to actually acknowledge the contribution that people might be making to the firm in other ways. If they don't, then the associates and ... [other] staff become quite cynical that ... [what] we are saying in terms of ... our commitment to corporate social responsibility is all about PR and nothing else.

If research on financial incentives and business frames is correct, the cultural importance of financial incentives may influence professional judge-

402

ment in risky and sometimes subconscious ways.[60] Even amongst those downplaying the significance of incentives, there were some clues that they had reservations about the context within which they and their firms operated. They tended to support a view that things were changing: younger staff were sometimes 'a bit gung-ho doing things that we're very uncomfortable [with]' (PP2), their 'instincts are sound but [their] experiences are weak' (PP5). The increasingly cut-throat lateral-hiring market for partners was also blamed for diminishing cultures of ethics; loyalty was more short-term and the concern for reputation less strong:

> ... they are out to make as much money as they can. And I don't think they put the reputation of the firm as highly as I do.
> (PP4)

Contextual pressures were not generally offset by significant counter-balances: 'in the training we give, [ethics] doesn't feature very highly' (PP4). Some private practice firms did have some infrastructure for taking ethics matters more seriously but an ethical culture tended to be assumed rather than actively fostered. '[T]one from the top' (PP1) and the idea that the unethical would get caught out were frequently mentioned. Also, firms were reliant on choosing the 'right' people: 'The best solution though is that you've got to trust the people and employ the right people which reflect the firm's ethos ...' (PP1). Whether a culture of trust was a coherent or robust response to such pressures was doubted by some:

> there's a big difference between deeds and words ... [We have] a set of values for the organization ... which are kind of inculcated at every point, but the ... difficulty ... always is ... Are they truly embedded? Are they truly how the company operates? Or are they again, a fig leaf ...? ... much is ... observed in the breach rather than ... in the real practice.
> (IH10)

As others have noted,[61] the view could also be different from the top and the bottom of an organization:

> I don't think I've ever come across any support or encouragement on [the ethics] front ... it's assumed that you've ... gone through your ethics training ... and you are meant to know it all. Nothing has ever, really ever, been said to me ... from the partners or in terms of training that in any way encourages it or supports it.
> (PP6)

It seems, therefore, fair to say that for our respondents the infrastructure for ensuring ethicality was limited. A number would say this was on the basis that such infrastructure was largely unnecessary.

60 For example, Kouchaki et al., op. cit., n. 58.
61 See references at nn. 40–42, above.

4. *An example of contextual pressures? The billing scenario*

The last section of our interviews involved short ethical dilemmas to which respondents were asked how they would and should respond. They were reassured there was no necessarily correct answer to any problem.

The vignettes discussed here were adapted from tools used with lawyers and law students in Australia.[62] They were designed to draw out key ethical issues facing lawyers in a variety of practice situations. Offering an encouragement to think in the moment, and to examine the ideas and values at play when the problems were discussed, the vignettes were an integral part of our approach. Here we discuss the two ethical scenarios most likely to fall within the ordinary experience of commercial lawyers. Firstly, a billing scenario relevant to the tension between client and personal/business interests:

> Imagine you are an associate in a law firm; your supervising partner meets a regular client, and provides an estimate of £20,000 for the work on what he assesses as a complicated matter. The client is usually billed on an hourly fee basis. The partner gives the matter to you to progress, and you find it less complex following some changes in the client's situation and you finish the work much earlier than expected. It then comes to your attention that the client has still been billed for £20,000. The client is delighted that the work has been completed ahead of time and he's happy with the bill. Can I ask you what would you do in that situation?

The aim of the problem was to suggest contractual ambiguity on what the agreed billing arrangement was. As drafted, the £20,000 appears to be only an estimate and not a quote. In professional terms there is less ambiguity; a lawyer is supposed to put the client's position before his or her own. In a situation of ambiguity, one might expect the client's interest to be put first. How did our respondent interpret the problem?

It was mostly in-house practitioners that said because an *estimate* was given, then billing the £20,000 was probably wrong. Those assuming it was a fixed fee had been agreed tended to be in private practice. Although the numbers of interviews we conducted was small, the difference was striking. Both groups tended to interpret an ambiguity in the facts of the question in a self-interested manner: the in-housers' natural perspective would have been as a client (although they would have experience of billing situations from when they were in private practice), the private practitioners as billers.

Almost all our respondents proceeded on the assumption that the partner would not be receptive to an argument that the bill was not appropriate. PP4 said:

---

62 The Queensland Ethics Survey, at <http://www.lsc.qld.gov.au/ethics-checks/surveys>; J. Palermo and A. Evans, 'Zero Impact: Are Lawyers Values Affected by Law School?' (2005) 8 *Legal Ethics* 240. A third vignette not applicable to the commercial context and so less illuminating to this article was also used.

> [T]he partner would have explained that . . . 'you win on some of these and you lose on some of these'. And having agreed a fee with the client, I think that the partner would say, we are going to charge that amount.

PP4 appears to ignore ambiguity (whether a fee has been agreed) in favour of the firm: the fee is assumed to have been agreed. Others picked up an ambiguity but, almost without exception, their approach to resolution was by reference to the partner rather than the client: that is, the associate should raise it with the partner. Some indicated that if the partner did not provide a satisfactory explanation then it would need to be taken further with (say) the Senior Partner, although that too was a rare response.

Different values appeared to be at work when our respondents discussed this approach. The notion of a trusted relationship with the client was shaped within the context of the business interests of the firm and the hierarchy within it. Few said they should discuss it with the client, and thought that unlikely to occur in actual practice.

Even where there was more willingness to assist the client, this was framed not in ethical terms but in terms of the firm's business interest, as an opportunity to protect and promote the reputation of the firm. A case has to be made in terms of the firms' reputation and business:

> . . . I think both for professional reasons and actually for good business reasons it makes sense . . . why don't we charge them 10k? . . . they'll be bounding back to us with more business.
> (IH10)

They then need to conform to the social hierarchy of the firm and how action threatened the security of the associate:

> . . . well I know what they will do [laughs] . . . is keep their mouth shut, and not look like idiots . . . because . . . they don't want to lose the firm money and look like people who want to give it away . . . you do that at some risk to yourself . . .
> (IH10)

Even the suggestion of offering the client a reduction was thought to pose a risk to the associate's status within the firm. IH12 said '. . . it would be difficult . . . You might express surprise but you would only challenge it gently'. Another was blunter:

> . . . would I bring it to the attention of the client? . . . I'm also old and wise enough now I think to know that if I did that then that would be the end of my career at that firm.
> (IH6)

One way of coping with this tension between the client interest and the security and status of the lawyer was to frame the problem as a *business* decision for the firm or partner, not an ethical problem for the associate (or indeed the partner):

> the decision on billing, is ultimately the partner's decision, it's the partner's client . . . that is entirely between the partner and the client . . . I wouldn't do anything.
> (PP6)

Similarly PP8: 'it wouldn't have been my place to ... the business belongs to the partners and they are the one liaising with the client and agreeing the fee.' PP9 suggested raising it with the partner and suggesting a fee of £15,000 to leave the client 'more delighted'. They also provided an interesting insight into how they thought the partner would respond. The centrality of economics and the link between money and reputation within the firm was emphasized:

> ... it would very much depend on the partner in question ... what pressure that individual partner was under ... if their billings were down then it could be that they were putting their own personal standing within the firm above what was in the best interests of the client and what was fair to the client ... [even if I raised it] I can't imagine that it would actually come to anything.
> (PP9)

Notice below how this is seen as a matter of client management and relationships rather than of professional responsibilities. Arguments were almost always business arguments that spoke to the firm's reputation and the ongoing ability of the firm to make money.

Private practitioners were also more inclined to describe the relationship in contractual terms (and as already noted) preferring to see the relationship as a fixed fee or that ambiguity should favour their interests:

> ... it's open market ... time charges are simply an illustration ... unless you said to the client, 'it will be the lower of x and what we actually record'. That is a commercial relationship.
> (PP1)

That it is a commercial relationship implicitly excludes the professional dimensions of the relationship. Most spoke in commercial terms: 'I have no problem having a tough negotiation with a client on fees' (PP2). The same lawyer emphasized the need to be open and honest, but ambiguity, so often used to the client's benefit, is turned against the client:

> [U]nless you are dealing with a situation where you've got a clear and unambiguous contractual position where you can only bill on hours times rate, then I would be intuitively comfortable about that.
> (PP2)

Some assumed that the client would understand the full situation so there was not a problem. Another said that there was only a problem if there was a falsified fee note with the wrong hours, which 'strikes me as dishonesty' (PP7).

The language and approach suggests quite strongly that context and hierarchy do matter and that, on this occasion, ambiguity is minimized in such a way as to favour the firm's – and the individual lawyer's – interests, in tension with the client's. It was striking that in-house lawyers saw the tension immediately and did not minimize the ambiguity.

5. *A second vignette: being asked to do something questionable*

A second vignette looks at the tension between legality and client interests:

> You are an in-house lawyer acting for a company in a property conveyance. The rules are that before the property can be acquired by the company, a director's meeting must be held, minutes must be recorded, and written authority must be given to the director signing the contract. Just before settlement you discover that there is no document authorizing the company to enter into the transaction. You discuss this with the directors and they suggest you deal with it by typing up a minute of a meeting and then backdating it to show that they did have the required authority at the relevant time, so that the settlement can proceed. They say they simply overlooked holding the meeting and it's purely a technical matter and the deal is worth millions of pounds to the company. So what do you think you would do if you were asked to do that?

The vast majority of our respondents said they would not backdate, and most suggested they would find a work-around which involved holding an emergency meeting or otherwise ratifying the decision legitimately. Several respondents noted that pressure to do this was not uncommon (both in-house and in private practice) and that this was often accentuated by colleagues working outside this jurisdiction where backdating was, it was said, permitted. Mostly the reasons given for not doing so were straightforward: it was seen as a fraud or a breach of a lawyer's 'duty to the court' (although no court was involved):

> ... you have a duty as a lawyer not only you know, you're not just an employee of your company ... You're an officer of the court, you have a duty to behave properly. Falsifying documentation doesn't fall under that category as far as I'm concerned.
> (IH12)

The dominant reaction though was not based on professional duties but basic principles of honesty and the risk of criminality. For example, PP3 referred to it as 'producing a deceptive document' and PP5 as 'falsifying documents'.

IH5 described it as 'illegal' and 'bad practice' but also appeared to be influenced by the risk such activity posed to their own reputation and security: 'with computers it is so easy to tell when a document was created.' Lawyers were plainly happy to say it was 'just wrong' where 'there are plenty of other ways you can deal with the event you've referred to which are perfectly acceptable' (PP1). Some predicted a more genuine struggle with clients:

> You just can't. Backdating of documents is fraud ... [A]ctually ... I have had incidents like that... there's a nasty technicality ... an irritating one, and everyone argues 'Oh for goodness sake ... let's just imagine we did it' ... you can sometimes get under pressure particularly from clients who are just, you know ... hyped up, want to do a particular deal or something, and regard this kind of thing as just the kind of irritating legal technicality that ... gives lawyers a bad name and then get all angry about it.
> (PP2)

407

There might also be a risk that 'finding a solution' could lead to over-reaching as hinted at by IH10's comments:

> everything can be regularized by inventive minutes, um ... but again, um . . I mean ... if it's ... I mean ... if it can be done ... there might be a workaround there. But that is to record something genuine, not to create something that never happened.

Less black-and-white situations where documents were created after the event to ensure detailed compliance appeared to have occurred in the spirit of the occasion:

> ... occasions where ... people are together and they've talked about certain things and then we've um, you know, prepared the minutes several weeks' later to reflect that conversation and perhaps dotted the i's and crossed the t's in the minutes in terms of, you know, what we really wanted them to say ...
> Yes, we've done that, yeah.
> (IH3)

Here, the nature of the I's and the T's is opaque but it is an interesting indication of how the boundary between something which is clearly wrong and something which is simply helping clients get their problem resolved is dealt with through the benevolent interpretation of uncertainty. Whilst backdating is potentially fraudulent, the benevolent interpretation of ambiguity is a 'normal' part of the lawyer's skill. Some rejected this kind of approach:

> you quickly get into a kind of ... slippery slope of ... of misbehaviour which becomes increasingly difficult to prevent or argue against because with every little departure from the rules, you've got less to hang your hat on.
> (IH10)

IH2 said they would advise against it but not prevent it occurring, seeking clearly to extricate themselves from personal responsibility rather than stop the practice of backdating:

> ... I think I would probably get someone else to write the minute ... I would say 'Look, what you're proposing to do is [tantamount] to fraud, um ... and um ... my professional code of conduct doesn't allow me to um ... assist you in perpetrating that fraud'.

This concern with their own power and the tension to do the best for the company is clearly shown by his anxiety: 'even though it may ... bring me into a certain amount of disrepute ... you know, to be seen as an awkward so-and-so' (IH2). IH7 also saw his role as making his concerns known but not standing in the way:

> I would ... raise it as an issue with [senior in-house counsel]... escalate the matter to them. If I was asked for a recommendation, I would say that the firm's reputation is more important than this deal and that we shouldn't proceed to create notes and I wouldn't be party to creating notes.

Several in-housers mentioned they might need to take a reputational hit for resisting in this way. IH6 had his own long-term reputation firmly in mind:

> ... it's not just a case of dishonesty, you're making yourself a fall guy. So it would be very unwise to do what was requested because basically they're asking you to lie on their behalf, and carry the can, which I just wouldn't do ...

It was mainly but not solely in-housers who contemplated the possibility of backdating. PP6 was an exception, mindful that:

> I would feel I was taking all of the risk on myself in doing that. So I think I would refuse to do it. But then again you are weighing that up against the falling apart of a huge, as you say, multi-million pound deal.

And PP8 indicated that 'I'd like to think that I wouldn't but I can't help but think that in that situation there would be a lot of personal ramifications to consider.'

CONCLUSIONS

In many ways the interviews suggest similarities in the ethical consciousness of in-house lawyers and commercial private practitioners. The vignettes we have just discussed provide detailed examples of how institutional hierarchies and pragmatism may shape decision making. For some of our interviewees, ethical obligations in their code of conduct to put the client's interest before their own or their firm's interests and to promote the rule of law and the administration of justice were muted in their reasoning. Their discussions were richly infused with notions of hierarchy and reputation. In particular, where ethical concerns were recognized, these were often framed as reputational concerns to be made as part of a 'business case'.

The vignettes are illustrative of our broader point. For both groups of lawyers, ethical consciousness was, in important senses, narrowly drawn. This ethical minimalism occurred in a number of ways. Firstly, there was some resistance to the idea that ethical issues occurred with significant frequency. It followed that they thought ethics was not much relevant to what they saw themselves as doing.[63] Where specific ethical problems were recalled, interviewees almost always distanced themselves from those problems: other firms, clients, old employers, or other groups in the firm (young lawyers, if the partners were being interviewed; partners, if the associates were being interviewed) were responsible, or the problems occurred years ago and were rarer now. Ethics was something that arose elsewhere, at a distance, for someone else.

Secondly, there was a strong tendency to equate unethical conduct only with criminal illegality. Our respondents leaned heavily on criminality, and

---

63 We do not regard interviews such as these as being a good vehicle for exploring the frequency of ethical problems. There is too much of a bias against admitting to there being a problem (especially because one is dealing with elite groups). Nevertheless, as our interviewees proceeded, they began to recall some matters of concern.

dishonesty in particular, as determining the boundaries of what was acceptable. Consistent with a view that professionals might bias towards risky conduct,[64] some even emphasized the need to be *knowingly* involved in criminality or the need for conduct to be *clearly* criminal if it was to give rise to ethical concerns. If they are right to take this view, then it might be said that as regards their public interest facing functions, professionals are not held to a higher standard than ordinary citizens.

Thirdly, ethical consciousness was minimal in the sense that there was relatively little discussion of professional principles or (still less) professional conduct rules, either when practitioners were asked to talk about what ethics meant to them or when faced with ethical dilemmas. Practitioners often did not discuss, still less dwell on, the professional conduct dimensions to any problem. Where such things were mentioned, it was generally specific rules (the conflict rules, the rules on client money, the duty to the court) rather than general principles that they focused on. This is contrary to the intent of the current codes of professional conduct which emphasizes the importance of the principles.

A notable exception to this principle blindness was the idea that the lawyer should pursue the client's interests. This was recognized and emphasized by all. Many believed in the pre-eminence of this principle, a view contrary to the Solicitors' Code. Except for the specific example of the duty not to mislead a court, our respondents either ignored, did not know, or minimized the impact of that key part of their Code which emphasized the public interest in the administration of justice over the client's interest.

This brings us to our fourth ethical minimalism: the role of ambiguity. Ambiguity was a shelter from which lawyers' deflected criticism. It is possible to see ambiguity as something which creates a space for ethical judgement but this is not how most practitioners, especially private practitioners, saw it. For them, ambiguity diminished rather than heightened ethical relevance and played an important role in limiting ethical consciousness. Deciding when, whether, and how something was ambiguous influences an individual lawyer's decision to say no, to advise against or to facilitate the exploitation of law's ambiguity. We saw in the billing case study how ambiguity could be interpreted in a self-interested fashion and, in the backdating scenario, how ambiguity could be used as the vehicle for submitting to the pragmatic needs of a commercial hierarchy.

In this way, whilst Nelson and Nielsen saw lawyers using 'legal knowledge to serve the ideology and prerogatives of corporate management' as entrepreneurial,[65] our interviews suggested this kind of service was more standard. The active use of ambiguity sometimes gave rise to a sense of

---

64 See, for example, Langevoort, op. cit., n. 28; D.C. Langevoort, 'Chasing the Greased Pig Down Wall Street: A Gatekeeper's Guide to the Psychology, Culture, and Ethics of Financial Risk Taking' (2010) 96 *Cornell Law Rev.* 1209.

65 Nelson and Nielsen, op. cit., n. 19, pp. 469–70.

discomfort about bending too strongly to their clients' imperatives. They comforted themselves with the view that they were the client's agent, clients (or their employers) decided what constitutes acceptable risk, and they (not the lawyers) were ethically responsible for sharp practice or other problems.

Finally, we should reiterate that saying the approach of our interviewees is ethically minimalist is not the same as saying they are behaving unethically. The ethically minimalist position is consistent with the idea of the zealous lawyer, doing all they can within the law for their client.[66] This is not the place to rehearse all the arguments for and against the zealous lawyer paradigm but we emphasize that professional rules and principles are supposed also to act as a restraint on lawyerly zeal, and a minimalist understanding of those rules and principles significantly weakens the impact of that restraint. The rare articulation of obligations to protect the rule of law contrasts with a fond and regular conjuring of the client's interest. All lawyers, be they in-housers or private practitioners, were very clear in seeing ethical problems not principally through the lens of professional principles, but through the social and economic lenses of business. They were conscious of business and of law, but they were not much conscious of ethics as defined by their own profession's principles and they often actively resisted a broader notion of public interest.

In these ways in-house and private practice were similar. Let us concentrate now on some areas of difference. We cannot say in a study of this kind whether in-house lawyers are more likely to be unethical than private practitioners. Our interviews suggested in-house lawyers may be exposed more directly to pressure to push the envelope of ambiguity and – albeit in a small number of cases – they perhaps responded more flexibly to the backdating problem. The commercial and pragmatic influences of their organizations may well be stronger on the in-house lawyers, but they are far from weak influences on private practitioners. As we have noted already, some also had a broader notion of ethicality than private practice, and extra-legal notions of fairness might enter into the decision-making process explicitly. Corporate codes and a culture of ethical leadership, where they were in place and taken seriously by corporate employers or the in-house lawyers themselves, helped them take (they thought) ethical decisions although ultimately the balance to be struck remained the company's calculation not theirs.

Private practitioners could plausibly claim greater independence. They could walk away from instructions, or exit relationships, more easily than an in-house lawyer can walk away from their job, but they too have their own de-ethicalizing tendencies. The traditional notion that a lawyer is not morally responsible for advancing a client's ethically or legally dubious case, coupled with the idea that they were often advising on difficult, ambiguous

66 See references at n. 13, above.

questions allowed them more leeway to discount any notion of public interest in their work than in-house lawyers.

A final ethical minimalism was displacement. Ethical problems were generally a matter for their managers or employers not for them. In-housers' qualms may have been stronger because they were more often in the position of originating or managing legal problems than private practitioners (who simply received instructions). That role may have given them a stronger sense of their own agency (or control) over how legal issues were defined and managed within a corporation. Because in-house lawyers were more likely to suggest they had a voice in a normative (or business) judgement about whether risky activities were the right thing to do, their discomfort may have been higher. They were involved in the process of corporate decision making in a way private practitioners were generally not and this made it harder for them to disclaim responsibility. This may also have given them more opportunity to influence towards good than private practitioners who clearly saw themselves as technicians for whom such questions were not relevant. Equally, they may have just seen more behaviour of concern. This sense that the ethical lives of in-house lawyers are somewhat richer but more challenged may explain why some have begun to take a questioning position on the sector's identity and approach.[67]

Even though professional responsibilities cannot be delegated or displaced,[68] displacement can be a powerful force if a business demands something at the margins of lawfulness. Whilst Rostain suggested in-house lawyers had no compunction about saying 'no' to a client in the appropriate circumstance,[69] our data strongly suggests they put significant effort into avoiding doing so and achieved this with some dexterity. They did so, in part, to protect their own employment, status, and influence within the organization. Yet, private-practitioner dealings with clients were subject to similar, if less intense, pressures. And both seemed to be applying similar reasoning and tests to the question of what was permissible or impermissible. If this is right, the firm, and the 'market' are the main institutional influences on professional decision making, and ethical consciousness is not a strong part of professional identity.

---

67 B.W. Heineman, Jr., W.F. Lee, and D.B. Wilkins, 'Lawyers as Professionals and as Citizens: Key Roles and Responsibilities in the 21st Century' (2014), at <https://clp.law.harvard.edu/assets/Professionalism-Project-Essay_11.20.14.pdf>.
68 *Shaw* v. *Logue* [2014] EWHC 5 (Admin).
69 See Rostain, op. cit., n. 21.

Section A

1a. This article looks at commercial lawyers? The authors divide commercial lawyers into two different categories for the purposes of their study. What are these categories?
   b. The authors interviewed a "select and very senior group of elite lawyers". Why did they not interview lawyers with a greater range of experience?
2. What does the Solicitors' Code of Conduct say solicitors should do if faced with a conflict between their client's interests and the public interest?
3. In this study did in-house lawyers and private practitioner lawyers take the same approach to ethical issues in their work?
4. Is unethical conduct the same thing as criminal conduct?
5. Is unethical behaviour a common problem amongst commercial lawyers?

Section B

1. Do commercial lawyers see ethical problems as potentially occurring in business problems?
2. Should commercial lawyers see ethical problems as being separate from business problem.?
3. What is "ethical minimalism"?
4. Do you think commercial lawyers are more or less likely to act ethically as compared with other lawyers?
5. Should lawyers be more ethical than those who pursue other occupations?

Studying at University

University isn't all about studying. Most students want to make friends and have a good social life, as well as getting a degree. Many have lots of other goals, such as participating in sporting activities, travelling or earning some money. However, getting a good degree, and thereby opening up a really wide range of employment possibilities, often features quite highly on many students' wishlists. In order to achieve your full academic potential, and graduate with a degree that you really think reflects your true abilities, it helps to think about the study skills you might need to acquire, or develop, to help you. The purpose of this chapter of *How to Study Law* is to help you fulfil your academic potential. It suggests some strategies to help you study law more effectively, so that you can improve your academic performance, and also so that studying law may become a more enjoyable and satisfying experience for you, and one which leaves time for all the other things you want to do while you are at university.

▶ 9.1

Successful study does not simply involve spending a lot of time working. Students who spend a lot of time on their work do not necessarily receive high marks (although clearly there is some correlation between the effort you put in to your academic work and the results you can expect to achieve). The purpose of this chapter is to suggest some techniques which you can apply to the tasks which law students are asked to carry out, such as writing essays or participating in seminars, which will enable you to get the most out of the degree you have chosen to study.

LEARNING INDEPENDENTLY

As a student in a college or university, you will be expected to take responsibility for your own learning. Your tutors will assume that you can work on your own without supervision, develop your research skills, complete assessment tasks and hand them in on time. You are likely to spend a much smaller proportion of your time on timetabled activities than you did at school. Your tutors will generally be helpful, but they are not school teachers, and they will not expect to guide your day-to-day learning in the same way as your teachers may have done. You will be responsible for ensuring that you know what lectures and small group sessions you need to attend, where they are held and at what time. You will be expected to know whether you have to prepare work in advance of a seminar or tutorial, and to do it in time. You will also be responsible for meeting any deadlines set for coursework or assessment tasks. The freedom to learn in your own way is very rewarding, but some people find this approach very challenging, because it is extremely different to the one they were used to before they came to university.

▶ 9.2

It is up to you to organise your time and plan it so that you can get everything done which you need to do, both in terms of your academic work and your social life, as well as any paid employment you might be engaged in. The next section of this chapter is devoted to time management, because it is one of the most useful skills you can learn. It will not just be useful whilst you are a student; it is one of the skills that are commonly called "transferable", because it can be used not just while you are a student, but also throughout the rest of your life.

MANAGING YOUR TIME

9.3 As a law student, you will be expected to do a number of different things: attend classes or lectures, prepare work for discussion in tutorials, seminars or classes, write essays and sit exams. At the same time, there will be other things you want to do, such as go out with your friends, go shopping or play sports. There will also be things that you pretty much *have* to do (unless you can get someone else to do them for you) like buying food and doing the washing. In order to fit everything in, it's best to work out a plan, so that you don't forget to do something or start getting behind with your work.

- **Buy a diary or use the calendar on your mobile device**
  You can use your diary or electronic calendar to plan your time. To be effective, it needs to contain a complete record of what you have to do. You need to carry it with you and add new appointments as you make them. You could start by putting in all your academic commitments—lectures, tutorials/seminars, deadlines for coursework and so on. Then add in social engagements and other things you want or need to do. Get into the habit of writing other commitments into your diary or calendar as soon as they come up.

- **How much time should I spend on my law degree?**
  No-one would suggest that you spend all your time studying. The whole point of manag- ing your time is to have enough time *both* to study effectively *and* to do all the other things you want to do. It is impossible to tell anyone precisely how much time they need to spend study- ing. Everyone is a unique individual and has different requirements. But, if you are a full-time student, then think of working for your degree as being similar, in terms of time, to a full-time job—around 40 hours a week. At certain times, if you have an assessment to prepare, or exams to revise for, you will find you need to spend considerably more time. The important thing is to work out how much time you personally need to spend in order to fulfil the require- ments of your course of study.

- **Become good at prioritising**
  Much of the time you will have multiple things you need to be making progress with—seminar preparation, buying lunch, meeting friends, listening to music, attending lectures and so on. You clearly can't do everything at once. Many people find it helpful to make lists, covering what they want to get done on a particular day or in a certain week. Consider installing a list app on your mobile device. Get used to prioritising items on your list—highlight those that you absolutely MUST get done, and fit the others in around them.

- **Find out if there are hidden institutional time constraints**
  Even if you are good at time management, your plans can be upset by the arrangements made by your institution. It is all very well planning to do lots of research for an essay during the vacation, but not if the library is going to be closed for building alterations for three weeks. Equally, you may come across the problem of "bunched deadlines", where several of the courses you are doing require assessed work to be handed in on the same day. You can alleviate these problems by finding out about the library, computers, and other support services well in advance and by asking tutors to give you assignments in good time, but you

may not be able to overcome such difficulties completely. If you are planning your time well in advance, however, that should give you sufficient flexibility to deal with the resulting pressure on your time, and you will be in a much better position than someone who has given no thought to such problems.

- **Be realistic when planning your time**
  Although you will often be working to deadlines imposed by your tutors, it will be up to you to organise your time around those deadlines. Be realistic about how much time you need to set aside in order to complete your essays or tutorial preparation. It is counterproductive to set yourself a deadline that you cannot possibly hope to meet. Many activities will take longer than you think; for instance, most law students are surprised how long it takes them to do the research for an essay!

  When you are planning your time, you need to be realistic about your own strengths and weaknesses, too. If you are the sort of person who can stay in and write your essay on a Saturday afternoon when all your friends are going out together, that's fine. On the other hand, if you are the sort of person who cannot wake up before midday, it is unrealistic to plan to write your essay at 8.30 in the morning. If you do not allow yourself sufficient time to do something, you may start to feel depressed and frustrated. If your schedule is realistic, you will gain satisfaction from knowing that you have achieved what you set out to do. Of course, everyone underestimates the time they need sometimes, but you should try to avoid this happening to you too often.

- **Don't leave things until the last minute**
  This especially applies to preparation for tutorials and seminars, and the research you will need to do for assignments. If you leave things to the last minute, you may well find that most of the books and articles you need to use have already been borrowed by other students (and even e-books may have restrictions on their use). You can sometimes rescue the situation by finding the information you need elsewhere, but it takes a lot of thought, time and energy to discover alternative sources of information. Your tutors are unlikely to be sympathetic if you miss deadlines simply because you left everything to the last minute.

MAKING LECTURES WORK FOR YOU

Lectures usually last one to two hours, and are delivered to large groups of students at once. They allow the lecturer to explain the main ideas in an area. Often, lecturers will also take the opportunity to tell students about the latest developments in an area, and to explain any particularly complex parts of a subject. Lectures are often regarded as forming the backbone of a course and it is usually assumed that most students will attend them. The content of lectures, and the handouts or powerpoint slides that often accompany them, also form the basis for further independent study. ▶ 9.4

Lecturing style is closely related to the personality of an individual lecturer, so you are likely to come across a wide variety of lectures delivered in many different styles. Some will be excellent, some less so. As a student, you will need to develop a good technique for dealing with lectures, which you can then adapt to cope with the different lecturing styles you come across. Don't forget that while most lecturers want to be good at what they do, and deliver lectures of a very high standard, you are ultimately responsible for your own education. You must make lectures work for you. Here are a number of suggestions which will help you to do that.

● **Arrive in reasonably good time**
Important announcements are often given out at the beginning of lectures, and sometimes hardcopy handouts as well; you may be very confused if you miss them. Equally, the first few minutes of the lecture itself are important, as the lecturer will often summarise the main points of the lecture, or remind you where they have got up to in their coverage of a topic.

● **Listen actively**
Listening to a lecture can be a very passive experience. Students are not generally expected to interrupt a lecture by asking questions or making comments (although some lecturers will include interactive elements in their lectures). In a standard lecture, it is very easy to "switch off" and lose the thread of the lecture. To avoid this, take notes to help you to concentrate. Do this even if you are permitted to record the lecture: you may never get round to listening to it again, but your notes will be very important for revision when you come to do your exams. When you are listening to the lecture, try to relate what you are hearing to your existing knowledge of the subject and think how the new information fits into it. A lecture can be very boring if the lecturer has a monotonous delivery, but as an effective listener, you need to train yourself to ignore poor delivery, and concentrate on the content of what is being said, which you can briefly record in your notes.

● **Eliminate distractions**
In order to help you concentrate in lectures, you need to eliminate as many distractions as possible. Switch your mobile phone off; texting your friends might appear more fun than taking notes in the short term, but it won't help you when you are revising for exams. The same goes for Facebook! Make sure you are comfortable; use a clipboard if there is no desk. Use a convenient size of paper, which gives you enough space to set out your notes clearly. If you have a series of consecutive lectures you may become uncomfortable because you are sitting for long periods; try to move your limbs slightly during the lecture and use any brief gaps between the lectures to get out of your seat and move around a bit.

● **Take notes to aid concentration**
Since one of the main purposes of taking notes is to use them in the future, it is important to devise a system of note-taking which produces a clear set of notes which you will under- stand when you come to look at them again, weeks or months after the original lecture. Handouts or powerpoint slides that support the lecture can make the task of note-taking easier, if they are well used; they should show you the broad structure of the lecturer and the main topics which will be covered. The lecturer may help you by summarising their main points; they may also try to aid your understanding by including examples or illustrations; these are good to include in your notes, as they will help to remind you of the workings of the arguments. Note the names of cases, statutes and academic writers who are mentioned; if there is a lecture handout, this should help you as it will contain names of cases and statutes and other techni- cal legal terms, so you don't need to get all these perfectly during the lecture; you can insert them when you review your lecture notes.

● **Take notes which will be useful in the future**
There is no single "best" way of taking notes. Some people will take quite detailed notes; others will take down the key points in a diagrammatic form. Many people find it helpful to use headings and sub-headings to emphasise the main points made, and to indicate changes

in topics. Numbered points can provide a quick way of noting a large quantity of information. Underlining and the use of different coloured pens can direct your attention to particular points.

The most important factor here is to establish a style of note-taking which results in a useful set of notes for you to refer to after the lecture has finished. Since law degrees generally rely on lectures as the main source of information, you may feel you need to write down quite a lot in order to be sure that you have everything you need. However, don't attempt to write down everything the lecturer says, as you won't be able to do this, and you will lose the sense of what they are saying. When you have taken some notes in some lectures, it is worth stopping to ask yourself if they will be useful to you in the future. If they are too messy, too short or too confusing, you can take steps to improve your note-taking technique. If you are unsure about the best way in which to take notes, you should consult one of the study guides that are listed in the "Further Reading" section at the end of this chapter. You may also wish to consult a member of the academic support team in your institution.

● **Review your notes as soon as possible**
It is important to review your notes while the lecture is still fresh in your mind. You may need to expand what you have written, or add headings, or do a little research on a point which you have not understood. Some people like to summarise their notes in diagrammatic form at this stage.

TUTORIALS AND SEMINARS

Tutorials involve small groups of students who meet regularly with an academic tutor to discuss questions that have generally been set in advance by the tutor. Seminars are similar, but usually involve larger groups of students; sometimes seminars may be led by one or more of the students. These names for small group work are often interchangeable, so you may find something labelled "tutorial" which is attended by 30 students. The title is not important; it merely indicates a "teaching event" which is usually smaller scale and more interactive than a lecture. In both tutorials and seminars, all the students are generally expected to have prepared the topic under discussion in advance and tutors usually expect that all the students involved in the group will participate, by joining in the discussion. The following points will help you get the most benefit from these sessions:

▶ **9.5**

● **Ensure you know what is expected of you**
Many tutors set specific work for tutorials and seminars. Ensure that you obtain this in good time, so that you can prepare the topic properly. If you are unprepared, and unfamiliar with the subject matter, you won't get much out of the session, because you won't be able to participate in the discussion and you will find it hard to understand what is going on. Different tutors will run these groups in very different ways. You will need to be adaptable, to fit in with different teaching styles. Some tutors will make this easy for you, by having explicit "ground rules"; with others you will have to work it out for yourself.

● **Try to participate**
Often, you will attend tutorials and seminars with the same group of people for a whole module. Clearly, the experience will be more pleasant if the members of the group get on

with each other, but this is essentially a learning experience, so you have to balance your desire to be friendly with your learning needs. No one wants to make a fool of them- selves in front of a group of other people, but if you do not try out ideas in discussion, you are not going to develop your thinking, so a little bravery is called for. Try not to be so worried about what the others will think that you do not participate at all. Everyone is in the same situation, so people are generally sympathetic to contributions made by others.

- **Consider making a contribution early in the discussion**
  If you make a contribution to the discussion at a fairly early stage, it is likely to be easier than if you delay participating, for a number of reasons. In the early stages of discussion, it is less likely that other people will have made the point you have thought of. Tutors who are keen to involve the whole group may single out people who have not said anything and ask them direct questions; this is much less likely to happen to you if you have already made a contribu-tion. If you are less confident about talking in front of other people, the longer you wait to say something, the more difficult you may find it to join in.

- **Think about the art of polite disagreement**
  The aim of academic discussion is to try to develop the ideas you are considering. Often, this involves members of the group disagreeing with one another's ideas. Remember that you are challenging the argument which is put forward, not the person who is advancing it. It is also important to remember this when your ideas are challenged..Saying something like "Perhaps there's a different way of looking at this" is less confrontational than saying "I think you've got that wrong"!

- **Expect to be challenged**
  During group discussions, tutors will try to teach you not to make assumptions. Their aim is to help you to think critically and precisely. They will therefore challenge many of the things you say. Most people are not used to being challenged in this way, and the ability of tutors to question almost everything you say can seem unduly negative. However, if you are going to succeed in thinking rigorously, you need to be able to question your own ideas and those of other people, and tutors whose sessions are the most challenging may turn out to be the best ones you have.

- **Do not expect to take notes all the time**
  If you take notes of everything that goes on in a tutorial or seminar, you will be so busy writing that you will not be able to participate in the discussion. Not only will you not be able to say anything, but note-taking also detracts from your ability to think about the points that are being made. Try to limit your note-taking to jotting down the main issues raised and the outline of any answer given. You can then read over your notes later and follow up any points of particular interest.

- **Learn to take advantage of small group learning situations**
  It is much easier to learn in small groups than in large lectures, because small groups should give you the opportunity to ask questions about aspects of the subject under discussion that you do not understand so well. Clearly, you do not want to dominate the discussion, or inter-rupt with too many questions, but small group situations do give you an opportunity to raise issues that are of particular concern to you.

RESEARCHING A TOPIC FOR AN ESSAY/PROBLEM, TUTORIAL OR SEMINAR

When you are preparing for a tutorial or seminar, or preparing to write an essay or problem answer, you will need to carry out some research in order to find the information you need. In the case of tutorials and seminars, you will often be given specific reading lists, so some of the research has been done for you, but you will still need to use the information to the best advantage. Here are some suggestions to help you research effectively.

▶ 9.6

In this section we will use the following question as an example:
'How successful is the operation of section 1 of the Police and Criminal Evidence Act 1984 (PACE)? Discuss'

● **Read the question carefully**
Before you start gathering materials, you need to be clear about what you are being asked to do. Titles that invite you to "discuss" or "critically analyse" mean that you are expected to engage in reasoned argument about the topic; you are not being invited merely to describe something. Here, you are being asked "how successful" is section 1 of PACE when it "operates". So you need to know:

  ● That section 1 of PACE is about stop and search powers given to the police.
  ● "Operates" suggests you are being asked to think about how these powers actually operate in practice, on the street, not just what the statute says should happen.
  ● "How successful" and "Discuss" invites you to make a judgment about whether you think the powers work well or not when the police put them into practice.

One of the easiest traps to fall into is to fail to answer the question which is set because you are concentrating on conveying as much information as possible about the general area of law, rather than focusing on the specific aspect which is the subject of the question you are answering. Keep the question in mind the whole time; write it out and keep it in front of you while you are researching.

● **Identify your key words**
First, define the general area you are interested in. In our example, this might be "criminal justice" or "police powers of stop and search". At first, you may find it difficult to identify the terms lawyers would use to classify an area of law, so you might need to ask your tutor or law librarian to help you with this.

Now you know the areas you are looking for information on, you can look for materials in those areas. If you are unfamiliar with the topic, you might want to look for a textbook first, so that you can read it and gain some broad understanding of the topic; while you are reading, keep the question in mind and see how it relates to what you are discovering through your reading.

You may need to re-define your phrases or words if, for instance, you find that the first few words you think of bring up too many references. In that case, try to think of much more specific terms which you can search.

● **Use the references in the text**
In any good textbook, you will find references to other materials on the topic which is being discussed. If the textbook you choose does not have any such references, it is not going to

be helpful for your assignment, so choose another one. Academic writing, found in journal articles and books, contains a lot of references and footnotes. At first, this can be confusing, and you may tend to ignore them. However, when you are researching a topic, footnotes and references are an important source of further information.

A good way to start your research on a topic is to look in the footnotes or references of any textbooks, journal articles or specialist books that you have found; they often contain references to more books or journal articles, and you can make a note of these. Then you can consult your library catalogue and find out whether your library keeps copies of that material. Footnotes and references can direct you to other relevant material in a number of different ways:

(a) They can give full references to articles or books that are just mentioned or summarised in the text. This is useful if the material referred to is relevant to your work, because you can then read the full text.
(b) They can give references to other books or articles on the same topic, which put forward a similar argument (or the opposite one often indicated by the word "contra" in front of the reference). Again, you can extend your knowledge by following up the references.
(c) They can give further explanation about points made in the text.

All these types of reference can provide you with further information about the topic which you are researching. That is why footnotes and references are so useful.

● **Organise your research notes carefully**
When you are identifying the materials for your assignment, it is easy to lose track of what you have found. You get so involved in tracking down a potentially interesting article that you forget where you read the footnote which mentioned it, so you can't go back and find other useful references from the same place. This is very frustrating, so make sure you write down a note of where you found a reference, as well as the reference itself, so that you can easily get back to it. We talk more about recording your research in the next section of this chapter.

● **Use a variety of sources**
Searching the library catalogue will generally direct you to books with titles that include your key words. Most modern catalogues will also direct you to journal articles. Once you get an idea of the journals which are the most important in a particular area of law which you are interested in, you can locate them in the library or online and look through the contents pages of the latest issues to find the most up-to-date articles.

You can also locate books and articles by using any relevant electronic databases that your library subscribes to. Your library should have instructions about how these work; if it doesn't, you can ask one of the librarians to explain them.

You can use specialist law databases, such as Lexis and Westlaw, to locate both cases and statutes on a particular topic; they also contain references to some journal articles.

However, there are a number of specialist databases, such as HeinOnline, which concentrate on providing access to journals, and these are the best place for you to locate journal articles.

If you are researching a statute, you may also find it helpful to consult the website of the Government department which is responsible for the area of law covered by the statute, since Government websites often contain copies of consultation papers and other official documents which can provide useful background information and help you to understand the statute more easily.

There are a number of hard copy publications that give details of all British books in print, arranged by subject, as well as by author and title. The Index to Legal Periodicals will help you to find articles in legal journals and there are similar publications relating to social science literature, often called "Abstracts". Using these sources will help you find a wider range of materials than those referred to on your reading lists. You may then be able to use these as alternatives to the ones that everyone else is using or which are unavailable when you wish to consult them.

● **Be time-sensitive**

Start with the most recent literature on your chosen topic, i.e. the latest books and the most recent issues of relevant journals. These items may not appear on reading lists, so may have been missed by others.

If you are using a legal textbook (usually at the beginning of the research process), remember that new editions are produced quite frequently, so you need to be sure that you are using the latest edition. You can usually check this by looking on the publisher's website. Even if you have the latest edition, do not rely on it as your sole source of information; there may have been a lot of recent developments in that particular area of law, which are not referred to in the textbook, because they have occurred since it was written. Similarly with articles in journals: remember that the law changes frequently; check that any legal points made by the author are still valid.

● **Make the best use of your library**

You need to ensure that you are using your library as effectively as possible. There may be leaflets designed to help readers find their way around the different catalogues, or there may be a resource page for law on the internet homepage of your law department or the homepage of the library; see if any of these can help your research. Some libraries have specialist librarians who are immensely knowledgeable and helpful. There will always be someone to help with your enquiries. Try to help yourself first, but do not ignore the experts whose job it is to help you.

● **Use the internet appropriately**

Many students find the internet a very convenient source of information. However, it is unlikely that you can rely on the internet as your only research tool. And when you do use it, you need to use it appropriately. Many students just rely on Googling a topic, and think that this is sufficient. Google is often a useful place to BEGIN your research, but it is unlikely that you will find sufficient material if you just rely on Google, and do not use any other sources of information. You need to be aware that much of what you find using Google will not be appropriate for use in an essay or assignment which you submit at university. A lot of material on the internet is journalism, which is interesting, but not authoritative enough to be used in an academic essay. You should only rely on journalism or opinion pieces if that is the ONLY information you can find on a topic (which will rarely be the case). Thus it will only be very occasionally that you can directly use a newspaper article, or the opinion of a pressure group, which you have found on Google, to back up your arguments in a piece of academic writing. You will need to use the specialist electronic resources provided by your university, or look at a government website, or that of the Law Commission, to follow up the leads you have found on Google and build on those leads by retrieving academic articles and books on the topic you are researching.

However, if you go beyond just using Google, the internet can be a useful research tool. In addition to following up leads you find on Google itself, you can use Google Scholar to locate academic materials, and you can also use the internet can to find a range of official publications, published by government departments, or by official bodies such as the Law Commission, and such documents can be very useful for research purposes.

● **Researching for different approaches to law**
Bear in mind the perspective you need to adopt in order to answer the essay or problem question you are working on. Problem questions focus on a "black-letter" or "doctrinal" approach to law; they demand that you use decided cases and statutory materials to justify the points you make. In general, it is not appropriate to include references to other materials, such as academic articles, when writing a problem answer.

When you are answering an essay question, you may have the opportunity to introduce a wider range of materials; in addition to any relevant cases and statutes, you may be expected to discuss Law Commission materials, consultation papers and reports from relevant government departments, academic articles and books, and materials from other disciplines, such as criminology, sociology, economics or politics. You need to find out from your lecturers and tutors which approach you will be expected to adopt when you are writing your essay.

Our example essay title is clearly asking you not only to briefly discuss the relevant area of law (section 1 of PACE), it is also asking you to evaluate how well this section of the statute works in practice, and to do that you will need to find out whether there is any empirical evidence (produced by researchers who have, for example, gone and observed the police, or interviewed people who have been stopped and searched). Since this is a matter of criminal justice, you will find that criminologists have researched it a lot, and therefore you will need to use books and articles from the criminology section of your library to answer this part of the question.

● **Be prepared to search other nearby libraries**
Sometimes you may find that your library does not have sufficient information on a topic that you are researching. Perhaps everyone else in your year has been set the same essay, and there just aren't enough books and journals to go round. Think of other libraries in the area that you could use and have a look in their catalogues to see if it would be worthwhile visiting them. Perhaps their students are not all doing the essay on offences against the person that your year has been set. Often, universities have schemes which allow students of other universities to have limited borrowing rights; it is often worth finding out if one of these schemes applies to a nearby university library other than your own which you might wish to use.

● **Find things out for yourself**
When you are gathering and using written materials, remember that you must always find out things for yourself. The insertion of a footnote in a piece of academic writing that has been published in a journal or book does not necessarily mean that the footnote is accurate. Sometimes, when you find the article or case report that is referred to, you dis- cover that it cannot possibly be used as justification for the proposition which you have just read. In order to find out whether a footnote is accurate, you will need to look up the reference for yourself. You should never merely replicate a reference without looking it up for yourself.

● **Enjoy Research!**

Although researching is hard work, it can also be very enjoyable. It is immensely satisfying when you find some material which backs up a point you want to make, or you discover lots of information about a topic that you are going to write about. Researching is like many other things in life—the more you put into it, the more you get out. Give yourself a chance to enjoy your research by allowing sufficient time to do it and developing your research skills as much as you can—ask your librarian for help if you need it, so that you can learn how to find materials as quickly as possible.

RECORDING YOUR RESEARCH

Research can be very enjoyable and interesting, and it helps you discover the subject of law for yourself, but if you don't write down accurately the sources you find when you are researching, you can waste a lot of time. You will need to give full references to anything you want to rely on when you write an essay or answer to a problem question. If you do not write down the details of the material you find, it's very tedious to have to go back and try to find them again.

▶ **9.7**

● **Always write down a full reference**

Whenever you read something which you think might be useful, you should write down its full reference; this not only means you will be able to find it again quickly, it also means you have all the information you will need if you want to refer to it in a footnote and/or bibliography.

For a book, you will need the author, title, edition (if it is not the first edition), publisher, place of publication and date of publication. You may also like to make a note of the catalogue reference so that you can retrieve the item from the library easily; this will usually be a Dewey decimal reference number. Your reference should look something like this:

Bradney et al. *How to Study Law* (3rd edition) Sweet & Maxwell, London, 1995. (340.07 HOW)

If you are recording a journal article, your reference will be something like this:

Addison & Cownie "Overseas Law Students: Language Support and Responsible Recruitment" (1992) 19 JLS p.467 (PER340 J6088)

It is important to write down references in such a way that you can easily distinguish between references to books, and references to articles. The system that has been used here is to italicise the titles of books, but put titles of articles inside inverted commas. You may be told by your tutor what system of 'citation' or referencing to use; it is important to follow any instructions you are given.

● **Make concise notes**

Always begin by asking yourself why you are taking notes. Refresh your memory as to the question you are trying to answer. Remember that you can take different types of notes on different parts of a text—detailed notes on the directly relevant parts, outline notes on other parts, while some parts you will be able to read through without taking any notes at all.

● **Make clear notes**

Your notes will be more use to you if they are reasonably neat. Try to develop a standard way of recording the source you are taking the notes from, perhaps always putting it at the top right-hand corner of the page, or in the margin. You can use this reference for your bibliography, or for footnotes, or for your own use if you need to clarify a point at some later stage. In order to make it even easier to find your way around the original text, you might like to make a note of the actual page you have read, either in the margin, or in brackets as you go along. Here is an example of some notes on the first few pages of a chapter of a book:

H. Genn (1987)

Hard Bargaining

Oxford Uni. Press, Oxford.

(344.6 GEN)

Chapter 3 "Starting Positions"
Structural imbalance between the parties (p.34).
One-shotter pl. v Repeat-player def. See Galanter 1974.
Repeat players—advance intelligence, expertise, access to specialists, economies of scale. See Ross 1980.
Distribution of personal injury work (p.35) Pls huge variety of firms.
Defs-insurance co/specialist firm
Defs solicitors allowed few mistakes (p.36 top) Defs solicitors nurture relationship w insurance co. Contrast position of general practitioner.

The student who wrote these notes has not only noted the full reference to the book they are working on, and the main points made in Chapter 3 of the book. He/she has included a couple of references to work by other researchers (Galanter and Ross) which can be followed up later to see if those experts have anything to say which is relevant to the essay the student is writing. The student has also been careful to note down the page number in Genn's book that contains the points which are important.

● **Do you need to photocopy the bibliography?**
When you are taking notes, you will often note down references to other articles or books referred to in the text you are reading. You will have to decide later whether you need to look these up, but many people find that it disturbs their train of thought to look up the full reference for each of these as they occur in the text. If that is the case, it is important to have access to a copy of the bibliography of your source (on-line or in hard copy), so that you have a copy of the full reference in case you need to refer to it later. In the example above, the student would need to have access to the bibliography of "Hard Bargaining", otherwise they wouldn't know what they meant by references to "Galanter 1974" or "Ross 1980".

● **Keep notes and comments separate**
It is a good idea to think critically about the content of what you are reading. However, if you want to make comments, keep these separate from your actual notes in some way, such as by highlighting. Otherwise, when you come back to the notes, you might find it impossible to distinguish your great thoughts from those of the original author.

● **Good presentation is important**
Remember that clear presentation of your notes is just as important when you are taking notes for an essay or seminar as it is when you are taking lecture notes. Use headings and sub-headings, and remember that underlining and highlighting can direct your attention to particular points.

READING FOR RESEARCH

It is important to develop a strategy for dealing with the large amount of reading you will have to do. All students have to face this problem, but if you are studying law, you have a particular problem, because studying law requires you to read a great deal of material quickly. In addition, although by this stage you are an expert reader, you are unlikely to have had much experience, if any, of reading legal materials, such as case reports and statutes, so in this respect you are a novice again. When you are researching, you need to be able to read quickly through the material you locate, so you can decide whether it is sufficiently relevant to look at in more detail, and perhaps make some notes from it. **9.8**

The chapters in this book which deal with reading cases and statutes will help you develop an effective method of reading these new types of text, and once you have practiced, you will find that you can process them as quickly as other types of text, such as articles or textbooks, with which you are already familiar. There are many different ways of reading; for example, you can skim quickly through something, or you can read it slowly and carefully. In order to decide what kind of reading you should be doing at any particular time, you need to think about the purpose of your reading. You also need to be aware of the different techniques of reading and be able to use each type as it becomes relevant.

- **Scan the text first**

  To check the relevance of a text, skim through it, looking for the key words and phrases that will give you the general sense of the material and enable you to decide whether it is relevant for your purposes. When looking at a book, the title and contents pages will give you a broad outline of the information you will find. Sub-headings within an article perform the same function. You can use these headings to decide whether or not to read a piece of text in more detail.

- **Approach the text gradually**

  Even when you have decided that a particular chapter of a book or an article is relevant, check it out before you begin to take notes; you may not need to take notes on the whole chapter, but only a part of it; similarly, with an article. It is often suggested that you should read the first sentence of each paragraph to find out more precisely what the text is about.

- **Reading statutes**

  As you have discovered in Chapter 5 of this book, statutes must be read carefully and precisely. At first, they can seem very complicated to read, because they are so detailed. When you read a section of a statute, try to establish the main idea first, then you can re-read it and fill in the details on the second reading. You might find it helpful to copy the parts of the statute that you have to read, so that you can use a pen or highlighting to mark the main idea. There is an example below:

  Sale of Goods Act 1979 Section 11 (3)

  Whether a stipulation in a contract is a condition, the breach of which may give rise to a right to treat the contract as repudiated, **or a warranty**, the breach of which may give rise to a claim for damages but not to a right to reject the goods and treat the contract as repudiated, **depends in each case on the construction of the contract**; and a stipulation may be a condition, though called a warranty in the contract.

  The main point that is being made is quite simple, and can be identified by reading the phrases in bold type "Whether a stipulation in a contract is a condition or a warranty depends in each case on the construction of the contract". Having established what the section is basically about, you can now go back and find out what the section says about the effect of a stipulation in a contract being classified as either a condition or a warranty.

● **Reading cases**

Although reading a reported case might seem more straightforward than reading a statute, it is important to remember that reading the judgments in a case and extracting from them both the facts and the decision requires practice.

Sometimes you will be able to get an indication of the important aspects of a decision from a textbook or from a lecture. However, if you are faced with a decision about which you know very little, you can read the headnote first, which will summarise both facts and judgments for you. Many students are tempted to regard reading the headnote as sufficient, but this is not a good strategy; you need to read the whole of the leading judgment to understand the ratio of the case properly. (You will be able to tell which is the leading judgment by noticing from which judgment most of the points in the headnote are taken.)

Reading dissenting judgments is also helpful. It is a good way to understand the complexities of a legal argument. Often, your tutors will ask you to think critically about decisions; reading dissenting judgments are a good source of ideas about the strengths and weaknesses of a decision.

WRITING ASSIGNMENTS (ESSAYS AND PROBLEM ANSWERS)

9.9 ▶ During your law course, you will be set various types of assignment to submit to your tutor. The most common of these are essays and problem questions, and it is with these types of assessment on which this section of *How to Study Law* is focused. Writing an assignment is a challenge, but it is also one of the most rewarding aspects of studying law. When you focus on a particular area of law for the purposes of writing an assignment, you bring together a lot of the skills you are developing; you need to research, organise the material, reflect on the question and engage in some critical thinking.

● **Clarify the task**

Before you do anything else, read the question carefully. Identify which area of law it is asking you about. This may not be immediately apparent, particularly in a problem question. Read the whole question through carefully to help you understand which area(s) of law are involved. Then make sure you understand exactly what the question is asking you about the area of law involved. It is highly unlikely that it will just ask you to write down all you know about, for example, the tort of negligence. It is much more likely to ask you to criticise a particular part of the law of negligence, or explain the strengths and weaknesses of an aspect of the law of negligence.

● **Make a plan**

The next stage of the writing process is to make a plan. A plan provides a structure for your argument and allows you to organise your arguments into a coherent whole. It is a vital stage of the research process and you need to produce one as soon as possible. You may want to do a bit of basic reading first, but generally, the plan should be one of your first tasks. Plans for problem answers are easier to produce than those for essays, because the events that make up the problem give you a structure for your plan. In all cases, jot down the main points of your answer; later, you can refine your plan and fit in subsidiary points in the most logical places.

Example

"Discrimination in the legal profession is a thing of the past" Discuss.

Introduction *— much discrimination on grounds of both race and sex in the past- refer to numbers of women / members of ethnic minorities qualifying as solicitors and barristers, also women not able to qualify as solicitors till well into the twentieth century — see Bebb v The Law Society.*

First section *Currently, still a lot of discrimination on grounds of sex — refer to small numbers of women partners in solicitors' firms, small numbers of female QCs and small numbers of female judges. Also refer to research reports on women in the legal profession.*

Second section *Equally, still a lot of discrimination on grounds of race — refer to small numbers of solicitors, barristers and judges drawn from ethnic minority communities, also research reports on racial discrimination at the Bar and in the solicitors' profession.*

Conclusion *Although it appears there is still a lot of discrimination on grounds of race and sex in the legal profession, it is arguable that the situation is improving — use statistics to show increased participation in the legal profession by women and by members of ethnic minority groups.*

Your plan is there to help you; you do not have to stick with your original structure too rigidly. If you can see a better way of organising your argument once you have done a bit of reading, then adjust the plan. The plan in the example above is just a first draft. It provides a basic framework, but it does not contain enough ideas at this stage. In order to add more ideas, the student needs to go and do some more research and reading before amending the plan in the light of the additional information. However, this is a good start.

● **Reflect and evaluate**

When you have gathered the basic information, it is time to review your plan in the light of what you have discovered. Read through your notes, bearing in mind all the time the question you have been asked. Have you changed your mind about any of the points you want to make? Have you discovered additional information that you want to include in your answer? Where does it fit in to your argument? Now you will be able to make a new plan, indicating not only the main points you are going to make, but also any arguments or pieces of information drawn from your research that you wish to include.

● **Write a first draft**

Once you are satisfied with your revised plan, you can embark on the first draft of your essay. Before you start, read through the plan and make sure that all your points are relevant. To do this, look at the question again, and then look at your plan. Every argument you make should relate to the question you have been asked. This is what makes it relevant.

Here is an example of a first plan for an essay whose title is "Settlement of major litigation is a necessary evil." Discuss.

- Settlement definition.
- Settlement is necessary because a) saves court time b) saves expense c) saves litigants' time.
- But settlement is an "evil" because a) litigants are not equally experienced and do not have equal resources b) inexperienced litigants often go to lawyers who are not special-ists in the relevant field & are not well advised c) inexperienced litigants can easily be put under pressure, e.g. by payment into court, delays (often manufactured by the other side), worries about cost, risk-aversion.
- Conclusion settlement is a necessary evil, but currently is so evil it is immoral and unacceptable.

Every point that is made relates directly to the quotation that is under discussion. This is an initial plan. After some research, you would be able to expand some points, and to insert the names of books or articles that you could use to justify the points being made. But you would still ensure that everything related to the quotation that you had been asked to discuss.

- **Remember the audience you are writing for**
  When you write an academic essay in law, you can assume that you are writing for a reason-ably intelligent reader who knows almost nothing about your subject. That means you have to explain clearly every step of your argument. At first, many students are ignorant of this convention. They know their essay is going to be marked by an expert, so they do not bother to include all the information about a topic, only to be told by their tutor "I cannot give you credit for anything, unless it is written down in your essay. It's no use keeping things in your head".

- **Acknowledge your sources / avoid plagiarism**
  During the course of your writing, you will often put forward arguments and ideas that you have discovered in books or articles. If you do this, you must acknowledge that the idea is not an original one. You can do this expressly in the text by saying something like "As Bradney argues in 'How to Study Law'". Or you can use a footnote to indicate the source of the idea. What you must not do is pass off someone else's idea as if it were something you had thought of for yourself. That is stealing their idea, and it is a practice known as plagiarism. In academic life, where people's ideas are of the utmost importance, plagiarism is regarded as a form of cheating, and you will find there are severe penalties if your work is found to be plagiarised. In order to avoid this, you must always acknowledge the source of your argument. Students often worry about doing this, thinking that their work will not be 'original'. But originality lies in the way you put together your argument, not just in what you have discovered. So do not worry too much about originality. The thing to worry about is making sure you have acknowl-edged your sources. In time, you will use other people's ideas as a base from which to develop thoughts of your own, acknowledging their idea, and then going on to say something original about them. But it takes time to learn enough about your subject to do this. It is the sort of thing you can expect to be doing in the final year of your study, but not really at the beginning! This is the kind of critical thinking which you are trying to develop over time.

- **Do not make assertions**
  In academic writing, you must <u>always</u> be able to justify what you say. You cannot make asser-tions (an assertion is when someone says "X is the case", but provides no justification that proves that X is the case). You must always be able to provide reasons for your statements;

in an essay, this is done by providing a reference or footnote. In a problem question, all the points of law you make need to be substantiated by a reference to some legal authority—usually the ration of a case, or a section of a statute.

Example

If someone writes "Small claims are proceedings involving £5,000 or less" that is an assertion. There is no evidence that the statement is true, the author is just expecting us to take their word for it. After a little research, it is possible to rewrite the sentence so as to include the evidence which proves the statement: "Under Part 26.6 of the Civil Procedure Rules, small claims are proceedings involving £5,000 or less." Alternatively, you could include the justification in a footnote. Then the statement would look like this:
Small claims are proceedings involving £5,000 or less.[1]

----
[1]   Civil Procedure Rules 26.6.

● **Consider the style of your writing**

   An academic essay is a formal piece of writing, so the style in which you write should not be too colloquial. Shortened forms of phrases, such as isn't and mustn't, are inappropriate. However, pomposity is equally inappropriate. Phrases such as "I submit that. . ." are out of place. Advocates make submissions in court, but you do not make submissions in an academic essay, even in a law school!

   Aim for a clear, direct style, which conveys your arguments in a way which can be readily understood. Use paragraphs to indicate a change of subject, and keep sentences reasonably short. In general, academic writing is written in an impersonal style, so writers do not use phrases such as "I think that. . .". They use alternative, less personal, phrases, such as "This indicates that. . ."

● **Be prepared to write several drafts**

   Before you arrive at the final version of your essay, you should have produced several drafts. You should read each draft carefully, making additions and alterations that you then incorporate into the next draft. Although it is important to correct the spelling and the grammar in each draft, the primary reason for having several drafts is to give yourself the opportunity to examine your argument and make sure that it is as clear and convincing as possible. Think about what you are saying. Have you justified all the points you have made? Does the argument flow logically from one point to another? Is the material relevant?

● **Do not describe too much**

   In general, the object of writing academic essays is to engage in critical analysis, i.e. thought and argument. Your tutors are not looking for detailed descriptions of subjects that they could, after all, read in any competent textbook. A certain amount of description is necessary, to explain what you are talking about, but the main emphasis in any academic piece of work will be on analysing. You are interpreting for the reader the significance of what you have described, and it is this process that is most important.

● **A few points about problem answers**
It is often said that it is easier to answer a problem than to write an essay, but this is largely a matter of personal preference. Problem answers are certainly easier in one sense because they provide a framework for your answer by posing certain issues that you must cover. The research and planning process described above will help you when you are answering a problem question, just as much as an essay.

Problem answers do not need lengthy introductions. The convention is that you need to introduce a problem answer by identifying the main issue in the problem. Whenever you make a statement about the law, you must give the relevant legal authority; for example, "When X wrote to Y saying that if he did not hear from Y, he would assume that Y agreed to the contract, this has no legal effect, because silence does not imply consent (Felthouse v Bindley (1862) 11 C.B. 869)."

Remember that socio-legal information is not usually relevant in a problem answer. Strictly speaking, problem questions are just asking you to identify the relevant legal rules relating to the issues raised. There may be very interesting research studies on a topic, but these are not relevant to a problem answer.

EXAMS AND ASSESSMENT

9.10 ▶ It is likely that you will experience a number of different forms of assessment, including continuous assessment, based on written work submitted during the course of the academic year, and the traditional three-hour unseen examination. The strategies discussed above will help you to cope with the various forms of continuous assessment which you are likely to meet. This section will therefore concentrate on strategies designed to help you cope with the traditional unseen examination.

● **Make a revision timetable in good time**
It is important to make a realistic revision timetable well in advance of the examinations, allocating a certain amount of time for each subject you have to prepare. Most people find it best to study all their subjects concurrently, doing a bit of each one in turn, rather than finishing one before going on to the next one, which brings the danger that you might never get round to the last subject.

● **Reduce your notes to a manageable size**
At the beginning of the revision period, you are likely to find that you have a large amount of notes. It is a good idea to reduce the size of these, by taking even briefer notes from your original notes, so that you end up with a manageable quantity of material to work with. As the examinations approach, most people reduce their notes again, perhaps several times, so that a whole topic can be covered comprehensively, but speedily.

● **Question-spotting is a risky strategy**
It is sensible to consider what sort of subjects might come up in the examination. Consulting old examination papers is a useful way of finding out what is expected of you in the exam. However, it is unwise to "question spot" too precisely. It is unlikely that you will be able to revise the whole course; indeed, this would often be a waste of effort, but you need to cover several subjects in addition to the three or four which you hope will come up, so that you have plenty of choice when it comes to deciding which questions you will answer in the examination. Being familiar with a range of subjects is a sensible strategy because:

(a) Your favourite topics might not come up at all.
(b) Some topics might come up, but in a way which is unfamiliar to you.
(c) Your favourite topic might be mixed up with another topic which you have not revised.

● **Consider practising timed answers**
If you find it difficult to write answers quickly, it is a good idea to practice writing some answers in the same time that you will have in the examination. Use questions from old examination papers.

● **Make sure you get enough rest**
Studying hard for examinations is a very tiring experience. Try to ensure that you get sufficient sleep and exercise, so that you remain as fresh as possible. Burning the midnight oil is not necessarily a sensible strategy.

● **Feel as comfortable as possible during the exam**
Before you enter the examination room, make sure you have all the pens, pencils and so on that you need. Wear something comfortable, preferably several layers of clothing so you can discard some if the room is hot, or add additional layers if you are cold. Check whether you are allowed to take drinks or food into the examination room. If you are allowed to do so, it is a matter of personal choice whether you take advantage of this facility or not; some people find it helps to have a can of drink, others find it a distraction. Check that you know where you have to sit, and whether there are any attendance slips or other forms that you have to fill in. Ensure that you know whether or not you will be told when you can start the examination; you do not want to sit there, waiting for an instruction that never comes.

● **Read the instructions on the exam paper very carefully**
Make sure that you read the instructions at the top of the examination paper very carefully. The paper may be divided into different sections and frequently candidates must answer a certain number of questions from each section. Sometimes you will be asked to write certain questions in certain answer books. Always make sure that you comply with any instructions of this kind; the examiner may not give you any marks for material you have written in contra-vention of such instructions.

● **Develop good examination technique**
In the examination, plan your time carefully. Provided that all the questions carry an equal number of marks, you should allow an equal amount of time for answering each question. Sub-divide your time into reading the question, planning the answer, writing the answer and checking it. Planning is a very important part of good examination technique. If you spend a few minutes setting out a good plan, it will allow you to write a much fuller answer than if you are thinking out your answer as you go along, because all the basic thinking will be done at the planning stage, and you will be able to concentrate on writing a relevant answer. Do not spend more than the time that you have allocated for each question. If you run out of time, leave that question and go on to the next one, returning to the unfinished question if you have some spare time later.

● **Answer the question**

Read the question carefully. To gain the maximum number of marks, your answer must be relevant to the question you have been asked. If you are familiar with a topic on which a question is set, it is tempting to write down a version of your notes, which includes all you know about that topic, in the hope that you will get a reasonable number of marks. However, if you merely write all you happen to know about a topic, it is unlikely that you will be answering the question. You need to slant your information to the question, showing how the things you know relate to the precise question that you have been asked.

● **Answer the correct number of questions**

Under pressure of time, some people fail to answer the whole examination paper by missing out a question. Examiners can only award marks for what is written on the examination paper. By not answering a question, you have forfeited all the marks allocated to that question. However, it is often said that the easiest marks to gain are the ones awarded for the beginning of an answer, so if you do run out of time, it is much better to use those final minutes to start the final question, rather than perfecting answers you have already finished.

● **Remember that examiners are human, too**

When you are writing an examination paper, you often feel as if the examiner is the enemy "out there", determined to catch you out. In fact, examiners do not want candidates to fail. They generally expect students who have done a reasonable amount of work to pass examinations.

INTERNATIONAL STUDENTS

9.11 ▶ The study skills discussed in this chapter are required by all law students. However, if English is not your first language you may feel that you would like some extra assistance with studying in the UK. Most institutions which welcome students from around the world have a support service which offers different classes covering a range of English Language and study skills, and you should try and find out about these at an early stage in your course. Even if your English is very good, you might be able to pick up some useful tips about studying in the UK from such classes. The support service will also be able to help you familiarise yourself with the particular types of teaching and learning situations which you will find in British educational institutions, what might be termed the "hidden culture" of learning, such as particular ways of writing essays or behaving in seminars, which might be different to those with which you are familiar at home. This sort of information can be very useful, as it is impossible to discover beforehand, however good your English is. Many institutions also offer self-access materials, which you can go and use at a time that is convenient for you.

Further reading

If you would like to find out more about any of the topics covered in this chapter, you will find that there are many books on study skills available. The following book covers a wide range of study skills.

S. Cottrell, *The Study Skills Handbook*, 4th edn, Palgrave Macmillan, (2013).

You will find that this author, Stella Cottrell, has also written a large number of other books on specific aspects of studying at university, which you might also find helpful.

There is also a series of books called "Pocket Study Skills", published by Palgrave Macmillan. You might find some of the titles in that series useful in giving you hints and tips about particular aspects of study skills. Titles in this series which you might find helpful include:

Brilliant Writing Tips for Students
Getting Critical
Planning Your Essay
Reading and Making Notes
Referencing and Understanding Plagiarism
Writing for University
Time Management

Exercise 6

STUDY SKILLS

9.12 ▶ The exercises below concentrate on some of the most important study skills which you will need at college or university. They may help you decide if these are areas you need to improve in order to get the most out of your course.

Note-Taking
You will find that you have to take a lot of notes, in lectures, and when you are researching for essays and other assignments. Being able to take very good notes as quickly as possible is a very useful skill.

1. For this exercise, you are going to take notes on the first three pages of the article entitled "In scope but out of reach? Examining the differences between publicly funded telephone and face-to-face family law advice" by Marisol Smith et al., which you will find in Exercise 5 of this book. Before you start, re-read the suggestions about taking notes in Chapter 9 of the book, in the sections headed "Take Notes to Aid Concentration" and "Take Notes Which Will Be Useful in the Future".

   Once you have finished taking notes, compare them with the two pages of the article you were working on, and assess your notes according to the following criteria:

   ● *Presentation* Can you read what you have written? Have you used underlining or highlighting effectively? Could you have used diagrams or lists?
   ● *Clarity* Can you remember what your abbreviations mean? Are there words or phrases which occur frequently that you definitely need to invent an abbreviation for? Have you remembered to write down the full reference of the article you are working on?
   ● *Content* Have you included all the main points? Do you have a full reference to any useful articles or other documents which were mentioned in the footnotes? Have you written down too much, so that your notes are not really notes, but involve copying out nearly the whole extract?

2. Find some notes that you took in one of your lectures. Now carry out the same exercise with them. Use the criteria above to assess how useful your notes will be to you if you need to refer to them in the future. Do they make sense to you now? Will you be able to refer to them when you are writing assessments or revising for exams? Have you noted down the references to any cases or statutes that were mentioned? How could you improve your notes?

Essay Writing Skills 1—using footnotes and references
One of the new skills you will have to master at this level is the ability to use footnotes or references in essays to justify what you are saying. Everything you write in an essay must be justified, and in order to do this, you need to include a reference to an appropriate document in your essay.

You can do this by including footnotes or Harvard-style references. These two styles of reference are explained below. The explanation is followed by an exercise to help you practice the skill of referencing. You should find out from your tutor which style of referencing they want you to use, and then learn to use it as early on as possible in your course, so that when you have to submit an assignment, you know how to reference appropriately.

Using Footnotes

It is likely that your tutors will require you to use footnotes when you submit an essay for assess-ment. If you use footnotes, your essay will look like this:

Historically, women were debarred from entering university law schools.[1] Today, women are to be found in larger numbers than men in university law schools.[2]

Note that the footnote number is inserted *after* the punctuation. The footnotes themselves are located at the foot of the page; look at them now. They contain the full reference to the work referred to, *including the page number*; it is very important to include a page number, so that the reader of your work can look up your reference and check that the material upon which you are relying really does back up what you have written.

You must adopt a consistent order for the information included in your footnotes: author; date; title; place of publication; publisher; page number.

Computers make it very easy to insert footnotes; in Microsoft Word, you will find a drop-down menu called 'Edit' or 'References'; you can then click on 'insert reference' and a footnote number will appear in the text. Practice inserting footnotes in a piece of text, so that you know how to do it *before* you have to submit your first essay.

Harvard-Style References

References can be included in the text (these are known as 'Harvard-style' references), so that your essay would look like this:

Historically, women were debarred from entering university law schools (Sachs & Hoff Wilson, 1978, 27–28). Today, women are to be found in larger numbers than men in university law schools (Law Society, 2006, 34).

Note that the reference in the text includes the page number at which you can find the material which is being relied upon.

If you use Harvard-style references, you <u>must</u> include a list of the *full* references to all the materials you have included in your essay. So at the end of this essay, the references would look like this:

Law Society (2006) *Annual Statistical Report 2005* London, The Law Society. Sachs, A. & Hoff Wilson, J. (1978) *Sexism and the Law* Oxford, Martin Robertson.

Note that the order of the information provided is: author(s); date of publication; title; place of publication; publisher. This order remains the same every time you write a reference.

Cownie et al., *English Legal System in Context,* 4th edn, (OUP) p.209.

---

1   A. Sachs & J. Hoff Wilson (1978) *Sexism and the Law* London, Martin Robertson, pp.27–28, 31–33 & 170–174.
2   Law Society (2006) *Annual Statistical Report 2005* London, The Law Society, p.34.

Reference Exercise 1

Here is a piece of writing about private security firms. Read it through. Imagine this is part of your essay. The footnote numbers have been inserted for you, but there is no content in the footnotes. On a piece of paper, write down the TYPE of material you would use to justify what you have said. The first footnote is completed for you as an example, to show you what to do.

Private Security
(adapted from Cownie et al., *English Legal System in Context*, 4th edn, p.209)

An increasingly important form of social control which has hitherto been largely ignored by those writing about the English legal system is the world of private security. Private security personnel are those persons engaged in the protection of information, persons or property. They are privately employed, have different legal powers to the public police, and are accountable for the exercise of those powers to a private individual or institution, rather than to the public.3

The term 'private security' is used, rather than 'private policing', partly to avoid confusion with the public police, but also because that term conveys more accurately the wide range of activities carried out by private security personnel in contemporary society, activities which go far beyond the policing activities carried out by the public police. The range of activities undertaken by the private security sector is very wide. It involves the provision of manned services – guarding, patrolling, transporting cash etc, as well as providing bodyguards, private investigators and involvement in the management of prisons and escort services.[2] Private security entities are also involved in the provision of physical or mechanical devices, such as locks, safes and cash bags, supplying electrical and electronic devices, such as alarms, video motion detection devices etc. and 'security hardware' i.e the manufacture, distribution and servicing of a wide variety of security equipment.[3]

It is impossible to obtain accurate figures relating to the number of persons involved in private security in Britain today. Estimates vary greatly, partly depending on the definition of private security which is used. Figures reported by the Home Affairs Select Committee in its 1995 report on the industry ranged between 126,900 and 300,000.[4] The 1999 White Paper *The Government's Proposals for the Regulation of the Private Security Industry in England and Wales* estimated that there were then a total of 240,000 individuals employed in some 8,000 companies.[5] All commentators are unanimous, however, in agreeing that the number of persons employed in the sector is growing rapidly and many have noted that it is probable that the number of persons employed in the private security industry is larger than the number of persons working in the police service.[6] Thus in terms of quantity alone, we are dealing with a significant factor in the criminal justice system.

The answers to this exercise can be found at the back of the book.

Essay Writing Skills 2—Avoiding Assertions

A common mistake made by law students is that in answering essay questions, they fail to *justify* what they have written. Writing a statement without providing justification for it is called making an "assertion". Assertions are completely unacceptable in academic law essays.

---

3   Reference to book or article about private security, which discusses what private security personnel do, and how their employment status, powers etc. differ from the public police.

Virtually every statement you write in an essay should be justified by reference to something which proves that it is a true statement. This might be, among other things, a reference to a case report, section of a statute, a particular page of an academic book (monograph), or a page of an academic journal article. In the exercise above the footnotes were inserted at appropriate places for you. In this exercise, you have to decide where to put the footnotes, as well as indicating what should go in them.

Reference Exercise 2

Read the following extract and identify the assertions that it makes. Do this by deciding where footnotes need to be inserted to support the author's arguments. Then, for each footnote, indicate the *type* of material which could provide the evidence which is needed (e.g. a section of a statute, a journal article, a Government document etc.). The first footnote is completed for you as an example.

> **Uncovering Crime**
> (adapted from Cownie et al., *English Legal System in Context*, 4th edn, pp.224–225.
>
> It is generally accepted that the number of crimes dealt with by the criminal justice system is less than the actual number of crimes taking place. This is because a large number of offences are not reported to the police, so they do not feature in statistics which record the number of crimes taking place. It is surprising to find that the police play a relatively small role in uncovering crime. Research for the Royal Commission on Criminal Procedure (the Phillips Commission) showed that most offences were reported to the police, either by the victim, or someone acting on the victim's behalf; many crimes were also reported by witnesses. When all these instances were taken into account, the researchers concluded that 75–80% of crimes are reported to the police, rather than the police discovering the crimes for themselves. This data is confirmed by other research studies, including research carried put for the Royal Commission on criminal Justice (the Runciman Commission) which found that the initial source of information linking the suspect to the offence came from the police in only 37% of cases.

Write down your answers like this:

Footnotes needed as follows:

Location	Content
After 'place' in line 3.	Reference to precise page of book or article discussing the fact that there is a large amount of unreported crime.

APPENDIX I

MOVING ON: FURTHER STUDY AND CAREERS

This short appendix to *How to Study Law* helps you consider what you might do after your course of study has ended.

From School to University

A1.1 ▶ You might be reading this book because you are studying Law with the idea of going to university to study for a law degree. Sources of information about degree courses can be obtained by looking at the websites of individual universities, by consulting official websites such as *http://unistats. direct.gov.uk/* or by looking at some of the readily available commercially-produced university guides.

Whenever you are looking at such information, one important consideration to take into account is that if you wish to go on and join the legal profession as a solicitor or barrister, you would generally be advised to ensure that your law degree is a 'Qualifying Law Degree' or 'QLD'. This means that if you obtain the correct grade in your degree, it will be accepted by the professional bodies regulating solicitors and barristers, and will exempt you from certain parts of their training requirements. You can find a list of all institutions offering a Qualifying Law Degree on the website of the Solicitors' Regulation Authority at http://www.sra.org.uk.

From Undergraduate to Postgraduate

One of the things you might consider doing after you have got your law degree is to do a postgraduate degree. Most universities offer a range of Master's courses in Law (often designated LL.M., which means Master of Laws). These are generally one-year taught programmes, during which you usually take three or four different taught modules in a specialist area, such as Human Rights or International Trade Law, and then from approximately Easter to September you write a dissertation on a topic of your choice which is related to your Master's degree.

The idea of taking a taught Master's degree is to allow you to specialise in an area of law that interests you, so that you can gain more expertise than you were able to do in your undergraduate studies. Obtaining a Master's degree can also contribute to your ability to differentiate yourself from other candidates when you are applying for a job.

If you really enjoy researching the law and academic work in general, you may decide that you want to do a PhD. In Law, a PhD is generally undertaken by people who have an interest in pursuing a career as an academic. It allows you to pursue a research project over three years, under the supervision of an established academic who is an expert in your chosen area. If you are interested in doing a PhD, you should talk about it with your tutors, especially the lecturers who teach you the subject in which you are hoping to pursue your research. They should be able to discuss all the options with you, and to signpost those individuals who could be potential supervisors for your chosen project.

Using your law degree

Having a law degree gives you many options in terms of career. Many employers regard law graduates favourably, and the employment rates among law graduates are high, compared with other subjects.[1] There are a number of websites which carry a large amount of information about careers for those who wish to consider all their options, and you may find it helpful to look at them at an early stage. Two of the main websites for students looking for law related careers information are *http://www.prospects.ac.uk* and http://www.targetjobs.co.uk/.

Legal Careers

Traditionally, law graduates wishing to pursue a legal career made a choice between being a solicitor or a barrister. Nowadays, the legal services market contains a wide variety of legal occupations; the most commonly found are legal executives. You might want to investigate all of these before reaching a decision about which career path is right for you. Here are some ideas about how you might go about finding out about legal careers.

Becoming a Solicitor

The Law Society represents solicitors in England and Wales. Helping members of the profession by providing a range of advice for solicitors, and helping the general public by providing information to help people find the legal support they need. The Law Society's website has an area dedicated to providing information and assistance for people who want to become a solicitor at *http://www. lawsociety.org.uk/careers/becoming-a-solicitor/*. The website encourages you to find out as much as you can about what a career as a solicitor is really like, and it contains a number of useful documents, including a comprehensive toolkit with guidance, tools and resources to help you find out about a career as a solicitor.

Becoming a Barrister

The Bar Council is the body that represents barristers in England and Wales. It promotes the role of barristers as being at the heart of the justice system. It has a section on its website especially designed to provide information for people interested in becoming a barrister: *http://www.bar-council.org.uk/becoming-a-barrister/*. The website includes profiles of practising barristers to give an insight into the lifestyle and culture of the profession, as well as taking you through the steps generally taken by those wishing to become a barrister.

Becoming a Legal Executive

Under the Legal Services Act 2007 Chartered Legal Executives are "authorised persons" undertaking "reserved legal activities" alongside, for example, solicitors and barristers. The Chartered Institute of Legal Executives is the professional association which represents trainee and practising Chartered Legal Executives. Its careers website: *http://www.cilex.org.uk/careers/careers_home. aspx* provides a range of information for those wishing to find out about a career as a legal executive, stressing its attractions for those who want to pursue a cost-effective flexible path to a legal career. Fully qualified and experienced Chartered Legal Executives are able to undertake many of the legal activities that solicitors do. For example, they will have their own clients (with full conduct of cases) and they can undertake representation in court where appropriate.

---

1   Walker and Zhu, *"The Impact of University Degrees on Lifecycle Earnings: Some Further Analysis"* (2013) BIS Research Paper No. 112 p.37 and Walker and Zhu, *"Differences by degree: Evidence of the net return to undergraduate study for England and Wales"* (2011) Economics of Education 117, p.1183.

Becoming a Paralegal

The term "paralegal" covers a wide range of roles found within the legal sphere of employment. The Institute of Paralegals is the oldest representative body of paralegals in the UK and has a useful area on its website which contains profiles of some of its members, to give an idea about what being a paralegal means: *http://www.theiop.org/about-us/some-of-our-members. html*. The website also contains information about becoming a paralegal, discussing a range of issues relating to the career path of paralegals: *http://www.theiop.org/careers/become-a- qualified-paralegal. html*. This includes information about who hires paralegals, what skills, personal qualities, qualifications and experience is needed, and how to go about getting a job as a paralegal. It also discusses how you can progress from being a paralegal to a solicitor and explains how paralegals can apply to become judges of First-Tier Tribunals.

Finding Out More About Legal Careers

LawCareers.Net is a website developed in association with the Trainee Solicitors Group. It provides information about how to begin your career in Law, whether you are looking for a training contract to become a solicitor or a pupillage to become a barrister or if you want to find out more about the paralegal or legal executive route: http://www.lawcareers.net/.

APPENDIX II

ABBREVIATIONS

The short list below contains some of the standard abbreviations that you are most likely to be referred to early in your course. It is not exhaustive. It will help you whilst you are beginning your study of law. The most complete and up-to-date list of abbreviations is to be found at *http://www. legalabbrevs.cardiff.ac.uk/.* This can be searched both by abbreviation, to find out what journal or law report is being referred to, and by journal or law report, to find out what the accepted abbreviation or the journal or law report is.

▶ A2.1

A.C.	Appeal Cases (Law Reports).
All E.R.	All England Law Reports.
C.L.J.	Cambridge Law Journal.
Ch. D.	Chancery Division (Law Reports).
C.M.L.R.	Common Market Law Reports.
Conv.(n.s.)	Conveyancer and Property Lawyer (New Series).
Crim.L.R.	Criminal Law Review.
E.L.R.	European Law Reports.
E.L.Rev.	European Law Review.
E.R.	English Reports.
Fam.	Family Division (Law Reports).
Fam. Law	Family Law.
H. of C. or H.C.	House of Commons.
H. of L. or H.L.	House of Lords.
I.L.J.	Industrial Law Journal.
K.B.	King's Bench (Law Reports).
L.Q.R.	Law Quarterly Review.
L.S.Gaz.	Law Society Gazette.
M.L.R.	Modern Law Review.
N.I.L.Q.	Northern Ireland Legal Quarterly.
N.L.J.	New Law Journal.
P.L.	Public Law.
O.J.	Official Journal of the European Communities.
Q.B.D.	Queen's Bench Division.
S.I.	Statutory Instrument.
S.J. or Sol.Jo.	Solicitors' Journal.
W.L.R.	Weekly Law Reports.

APPENDIX III

EXERCISE ANSWERS

Exercise 1

1. Treason Act 1351. See Schedule, Consequential Amendments para.1.
2. See s.5(1) and s.5 (2).
3. "Roman Catholic" is not defined in the Act. It is therefore necessary to see if any other statute has defined the term and if not if any precedent has defined the term. If not, and if it became salient in a case, the court would have to define the term itself.
4. See s. 3(1).
5. Yes, but only after the passage of this statute. See s. 2(1).
6. None but only after the passage of this statute. See s.1.

Exercise 2

1. The Act makes provision for "free childcare for young children of working parents and the publication of information about childcare and related matters by local authorities" (see the long title).
2. See s.7(1) and s.7(2).
3. See s.2(8) and s.1(2).
4. Yes. Section 2(2)(h).
5. No. Under s. 2(1) the Secretary of State "**may**" make regulations.
6. See s.2(2)(i).

Exercise 3

1. In the year 2016 in the Court of Appeal Criminal Division, this being the 965th case heard by that court in that year.
2. Having an article with a blade, contrary to section 139910 of the Criminal Justice Act 1988. The defendant was found not guilty of two other offences. (See paragraph 1)
3. Holding that when the defendant was in a second floor flat and the knife that was relevant to the prosecution was in a car in a car park below the flat the defendant could be said to have "had with him in a public space" the knife. (See paragraph 19)
4. On the basis of previous relevant decisions it was necessary to show that there was a "close geographical, temporal or purposive link between the knife which was in a public place and the defendant who was in a private flat" and that this had not been done. (See paragraph 19)
5. Possession is a wider concept. (See paragraph 17)

Exercise 4

1. "An order. . . requiring someone to lodge their passport with the court or with some suitable custodian, for example the tipstaff or a solicitor who has given the court an appropriate undertaking" (see p.398 16 paragraph).
2. a. No (see p 400 paragraph 27).
   b.   In Re B (Child Abduction: Wardship: Power to Detain) [1994] 2 FLR 479 at pp 483-484 paragraphs 24-27 and at pp 485-486 paragraph 28.
3. The court thought both imprisonment and making a passport order were examples of the use of coercive powers by a court (see pp 401-402 paragraph 33).
4. The Supreme Court in re W (Children) (Family Proceedings: Evidence) [2010] 1 WLR 701 held that in cases such as this a balance needs to be struck between the need for a child to give evidence and that child's welfare needs. (see pp.402-403 paragraph 38) 1773.

Exercise 5

1.) In-house lawyers and private practitioner lawyers. The distinction is made at many points in the article including the discussion of who was interviewed for the study at p.394.
   b.) Lawyers with less experience were "markedly" less willing to be interviewed according to the authors (p.394).
2.) Do what is in the public interest (p.398).
3.) In their conclusion the authors say that "[i]n many ways the interviews suggest similarities in the ethical consciousness of in-house lawyers and commercial private practitioners "(p.409). However in the main body of the article the authors do note differences between the two groups. For example they observe that in their interviews "[i]n-house lawyers were somewhat more likely than private practitioners to suggest the public interest came first" (p.400). They also note these areas of difference in their conclusion (pp.411-412).
4.) The authors suggest that their respondents did equate unethical conduct with criminal conduct (see, for example, pp.409-410 and pp.395 -396). However the authors note that the Solicitor's Code of Conduct is concerned with matters that went beyond the criminal law (p.398).
5.) The article notes the existence of such behaviour (pp.387-388). However the interviews in the study explore the "ethical consciousness "of those interviewed not their perceptions of the amount of unethical behaviour that occurs. Nonetheless the article does conclude that "ethical consciousness is not a strong part of professional identity" for commercial lawyers (p.412).

Reference Exercise 1

1. Reference to the precise page of a book or article that discusses the wide range of activities carried out by private security personnel.
2. Reference to the precise page of a book or article that discusses the role of private security in relation to the supply of physical/mechanical/electronic devices and"security hardware".

3. Full reference to the 1995 Home Affairs Select Committee Report mentioned in the text.
4. Full reference to the 1999 White Paper mentioned in the text.
5. Reference to the precise page of a book or article which discusses the growth in private security personnel and concludes that the number of persons employed in private security is larger than the number employed in the police service.

Reference Exercise 2

It is generally accepted that the number of crimes dealt with by the criminal justice system is less than the actual number of crimes taking place. This is because a large number of offences are not reported to the police, so they do not feature in statistics which record the number of crimes taking place. It is surprising to find that the police play a relatively small role in uncovering crime. Research for the Royal Commission on Criminal Procedure (the Phillips Commission) showed that most offences were reported to the police, either by the victim, or someone acting on the victim's behalf; many crimes were also reported by witnesses. When all these instances were taken into account, the researchers concluded that 75–80 per cent of crimes are reported to the police, rather than the police discovering the crimes for themselves. This data is confirmed by other research studies, including research carried put for the Royal Commission on Criminal Justice (the Runciman Commission) which found that the initial source of information linking the suspect to the offence came from the police in only 37 per cent of cases. Footnotes needed as follows:

Location	Content
After "place" in line 3.	Reference to precise page of book or article discussing the fact that there is a large amount of unreported crime.
After "witnesses" in line 7.	Reference to the precise place in the report of the research carried out for the Royal Commission on Criminal Procedure which discusses the fact that offences are generally reported to the police.
After "themselves" in line 9.	Another reference to the report of the research carried out for the Royal Commission on Criminal Procedure, to the precise page where the researchers' conclusions are set out.
After "cases" in the final line.	Reference to the report of the research carried out for the Royal Commission on Criminal Justice setting out the statistics referred to in the text.

APPENDIX IV

FURTHER READING

The number of books about law and legal rules increases each day. They range from simple guides, written for the GCSE student, to thousand-page, closely argued texts, written for the academic. Some are encyclopaedias; others are exhaustive surveys of a very small area of law. This short list of further reading is intended to be of use to those readers who want to take further specific themes raised in this book. The list is not a guide to legal literature as a whole. Readers who have specific interests should consult their library catalogues for books in their area.

▶ A4.1

Introductory books

J. Adams and R. Brownsword, *Understanding Law*, 4th edn (London: Sweet & Maxwell, 2006).
   J. Waldron, *The Law*, (London: Routledge, 1990).
G. Rivlin *Understanding the Law*, 6th edn (Oxford: Oxford University Press, 2012)

Books on the English legal system

F. Cownie, A. Bradney and M. Burton, *English Legal System in Context,* 6th edn (Oxford: Oxford University Press, 2013).
K. Malleson and R. Moules, *The Legal System,* 4th edn (Oxford: Oxford University Press, 2010).
S. Bailey, M. Gunn, N. Taylor and D. Ormerod, *Smith, Bailey and Gunn on the Modern English Legal System,* 5th edn (London: Sweet & Maxwell, 2007).
C. Stychin, *Legal Methods and Systems: Text and Materials,* 4th edn (London: Sweet & Maxwell, 2010).
R. Ward and A. Akhtar, *Walker and Walker's English Legal System*, 11th edn (Oxford: Oxford University Press, 2011).

Index

LEGAL TAXONOMY
FROM SWEET & MAXWELL

This index has been prepared using Sweet and Maxwell's Legal Taxonomy. Main index entries conform to keywords provided by the Legal Taxonomy except where references to specific documents or non-standard terms (denoted by quotation marks) have been included. These keywords provide a means of identifying similar concepts in other Sweet & Maxwell publications and online services to which keywords from the Legal Taxonomy have been applied. Readers may find some minor differences between terms used in the text and those which appear in the index. Suggestions to *sweetandmaxwell.taxonomy@thomson.com*.

(All references are to paragraph number)